Jaime J. Sucher

Shetland Sheepdogs

Everything About Purchase, Care, Nutrition, Breeding, and Health Care

Filled with Full-color Photographs
Illustrations by Michele Earle-Bridges

CONTENTS

3

SHOULD YOU BUY A SHELTIE?

An Intelligent Choice

The Shetland Sheepdog, or Sheltie, has often misleadingly been referred to as a miniature Collie, implying that the Sheltie was established by inbreeding smaller Collies to obtain the diminutive stature that characterizes the breed. In reality, however, it is believed that both the Shetland Sheepdog and the Collie are descended from the same ancestor. One line evolved into a larger breed, the other into a smaller one. This common ancestor is believed to be the Border Collie, which can still be found today herding sheep in the Scottish highlands.

In addition to selective breeding, the resulting smaller size of the Sheltie was due to the environment of the Shetland Islands, where the breed originated. The Shetlands, a small chain of islands along the northern coast of Scotland, have a rocky terrain and sparse vegetation and are frequented by severe storms. The harshness of landscape and weather has led to a perennial scarcity of food, thereby putting a premium on small, sturdy, domesticated animals. In fact, most of the animals found in the Shetlands seem to have shrunk from larger relatives into miniature forms. Besides the Sheltie, these

Beautiful, intelligent, loyal, and graceful are some of the fine traits associated with the Shetland Sheepdog.

islands are home to the well-known Shetland pony. Shetland sheep and cattle are also of lilliputian size.

The diminutive size of the Shetland Sheepdog is one reason it is quickly becoming one of the most popular purebred dogs in America. A smaller dog has little problem adjusting to the confined spaces of an apartment, yet the Sheltie's courage, loyalty, obedience, and herding ability make it an excellent dog for country life as well.

As the name implies, the Shetland Sheepdog was originally bred to tend sheep. In order to be successful in this endeavor, the Sheltie had to be loyal, obedient, and courageous. A sheepdog had to protect its flock from danger yet not frighten the herd itself. In addition, the sheepdog had to be hardy, independent, and able to protect itself from its harsh surroundings. The Shetland Sheepdog was bred to achieve the temperament needed for the job, and its thick coat gives ample protection from the weather. Through years of selective breeding, these traits have become synonymous with the breed and can be found in all of today's Shelties.

Shetland Sheepdogs make excellent house pets. They are fast learners and extremely obedient. They are small, easy to care for, and beautiful. They possess the perfect temperament to be with children and are equally

CHECKLIST

Considerations

1 Do you have the time, energy, and patience to raise a dog properly?

2 If you purchase a Sheltie puppy, would you be willing to change your schedule to meet the dog's needs? The needs of a puppy differ greatly from those of an adult dog. Puppies are not independent and require more frequent feedings and closer supervision.

3 Are you willing to devote some of your free time to the dog? Do you travel on weekends or take long vacations? Are you willing to travel only to areas where you can bring your Shetland Sheepdog? Although dogs can withstand the stress of travel fairly well, they are prohibited in many hotels and motels.

4 Do you understand the long-term commitment involved in owning a Shetland Sheepdog? A dog should never be purchased impulsively, especially because a Sheltie may live a dozen years or more.

5 Do you have a yard, or is a park or wooded area available where your dog can get its much-needed exercise? The Shetland Sheepdog is a small breed and can be comfortably housed even in a small apartment. However, Shelties are a working breed. Both their physical and mental welfare depend on getting sufficient exercise.

6 Finally, can you afford to keep a Shetland sheepdog? Aside from the initial expenses of buying the dog and necessary supplies, feeding may cost as much as $40 per month. Additional expenses include annual visits to the veterinarian (see page 11).

suited to be a watchdog. All these traits make the Shetland Sheepdog the ideal pet for a diverse range of people regardless of their living space or their age.

Whether to buy a Sheltie is an important decision. Lack of awareness of the responsibility of dog ownership can result in an unhappy relationship for both the dog and the owner.

Free-ranging dogs constitute a major problem in the United States as well as in many other countries. Studies indicate that this problem is due more to human irresponsibility than to a dog following its wild instincts. In the long run, this situation can lead to the outbreak of diseases from nonvaccinated, homeless animals. These facts emphasize the importance of responsible pet ownership.

After considering all the points, if you still wish to purchase a Sheltie, find out if a chapter of the American Shetland Sheepdog Association is in your area. Its members can help answer your relevant questions.

Male or Female?

Once you have decided to buy a Shetland Sheepdog, you will have to choose either a male or female dog. In this breed, little difference exists between the sexes. Both have about the same disposition and are of equal physical proportions. As with most breeds of dogs, the males are usually more likely to roam while the females tend to stay near home. The only time you might prefer a specific sex is if you are interested in breeding the dog.

Regardless of whether you select a male or female, if you have no intention of breeding, have the dog neutered or spayed. Because an alarming number of dogs in the United States are homeless, owners should take all possible precautions against the increase of unwanted animals. Spaying the female dog also avoids the messiness that will occur when she is in heat. A spayed female will be more likely to avoid breast tumors, ovarian cysts, false pregnancies, and other ailments. Neutering a male dog virtually eliminates the chance of testicular or prostate cancer. Note, however, that if you plan to enter your Sheltie in a conformation show, it will be disqualified if neutered or spayed.

Adult or Puppy?

While the choice of gender in a Sheltie may not be important, whether you buy an adult or puppy certainly is. When making this choice, keep the following in mind.

One of the greatest rewards of owning a Shetland Sheepdog is watching it grow from

The alert and sometimes wary facial expression that characterize Shelties can be seen in puppies as well as in adults.

an unbelievably cute, awkward, tiny bundle of fur into a beautiful, dignified, loyal adult. However, this requires a great deal of patience, time, and energy. A properly trained adult results from diligent attention by owners who gave their puppy understanding, love, and the needed thorough training. All too easily dog owners neglect their duties. The result is a relationship in which neither the dog nor the owner is happy.

For the person who does not have the time to devote to a puppy, selecting an adult Sheltie offers other advantages. A well-trained Shetland Sheepdog makes a fine pet. Mature Shelties will usually have little trouble adapting to a new household, thereby saving the new owners the time needed to raise, train, and housebreak a puppy. An adult Sheltie, by needing significantly less attention than a puppy, makes

Each puppy has its own temperament.

an ideal pet for the elderly or for a working family. The greatest drawback to buying an older Sheltie is that you may find correcting bad habits the dog may have already acquired to be extremely difficult.

If you are interested in obtaining an adult Sheltie, start by contacting a reputable breeder. It may be possible for you to buy or even adopt a dog that is too old to be bred safely. By doing this, you can be sure of acquiring a Sheltie

raised by a caring and knowledgeable person.

When choosing between a Sheltie puppy and an adult, keep in mind that raising a puppy will allow you to train it to the habits of your household. Adult dogs, on the other hand, need significantly less attention, which means less work, especially for an older owner.

If you are looking for a show dog, you have two options. First, you can purchase a potential show puppy from a reputable breeder and raise it yourself. This way you will have the satisfaction of knowing that you have done the job yourself. Alternatively, you can purchase a mature show dog. This way, you are assured of your Sheltie's quality and beauty.

Purchasing Your Sheltie

The first step in purchasing a puppy is to contact the secretary of the American Shetland Sheepdog Association or the American Kennel Club (AKC). Get from them a list of reputable dealers and well-established, registered Sheltie breeders in your area. Visit as many pet stores and breeders in your area as possible.

Visit each store or kennel to inspect the dogs and the conditions in which they are kept. The

Consider all of the necessary expenses before you buy your Sheltie.

time and effort you spend in finding the right Sheltie will save you trouble and heartache later on.

When visiting the kennels, keep in mind that the quality of your puppy will directly reflect the quality of the breeder. Conscientious breeders will make every effort to satisfy you in order to maintain their reputation. Always feel free to ask the breeder questions, regardless of how silly they may seem. A good breeder will be able to answer all your relevant questions and be of invaluable help in selecting your puppy.

Place the least emphasis on the price of the puppy. Never be swayed into buying a dog because it is cheap. The old adage, "You get what you pay for," is all too true when buying a dog. A bargain price may indicate the dog was raised strictly for profit by an

inexperienced breeder or that the dog is in poor health. A more expensive dog from an experienced and reputable breeder may save you a lot of future veterinarian bills.

You should also avoid Shelties from kennels not dedicated solely to breeding and raising Shetland Sheepdogs. Breeders who raise several breeds of dogs are not always knowledgeable about the special needs of each breed.

As you visit each store or kennel on your list, pay special attention to the dogs' housing. Be sure the surroundings are clean and that the dogs have room to move about freely. Observe the coat conditions and overall appearance of all of the dogs. Each of these factors indicates the quality of the operation. Once you have found a dealer or breeder in whom you have confidence, you must then choose your puppy.

TIP

Selecting the Right Puppy for You

At first glance, Shetland Sheepdog puppies look alike—adorable, tiny bundles of fur and wrinkles. Learn to see past this. Resist the impulse to buy the first puppy that catches your fancy (which is most likely the first puppy you see). As you observe the puppies, you will begin to notice subtle differences in their physical characteristics and their temperament. Though they may be only a few weeks old, you can use these differences to help you select the right puppy.

Choosing Your Puppy

Examine the puppy's coat; it should be smooth and shiny. Its eyes should be bright, and the puppy should be sturdily built. Shetland Sheepdog puppies should look alert and be slightly cautious, for they are herding dogs. In most cases, avoiding both hyperactive and overly sedate dogs would be best.

If you watch the puppies play together, you get an idea of their individual temperaments. Some may be bolder, others, more shy. The puppy's temperament is a good indicator of what the dog's adult behavior will be like. You can therefore select a dog whose disposition will fit your home life.

Another good indicator of the puppy's temperament is its mother's behavior. After all, the puppy inherits many of its behavioral characteristics from its sire (father) or dam (mother). Observe how the mother reacts to people. She should show no signs of fear and only the slightest amount of misgiving at the most. As herding dogs, Shelties are inherently protective. The dam may take a little time before she senses that you, a stranger, mean her and her litter no harm. This type of behavior is actually desirable in a watchdog. However, the dam should show no sign of aggression.

If the puppy appears to be in good health and of sound temperament, the next step is to check its pedigree papers. These papers are a written record of the dog's recent ancestry—a dog's family tree. All the show champions in its lineage will be marked as such. The pedigree papers will also show if the dog has had its eyes checked. Shetland Sheepdogs, like many other breeds, may suffer from hereditary eye problems. When a breeder has the puppy's eyes checked and cleared, they are given a number that is placed onto the pedigree. Never purchase a dog whose pedigree papers lack this number.

If the dog's pedigree is satisfactory, ask for the date the puppy was wormed. Be sure to get a written record of this to show your veterinarian. Do not be afraid to ask questions. A reputable dealer or breeder is as concerned with the puppy's welfare as you are. Also, do not be offended if a breeder asks questions about your experience with dogs and where you plan to raise your puppy. Take this as a sign of concern. In addition, keep an open line of communication so that the dealer or breeder can help you with any future problems.

Expenses

Though the initial purchase price of a Shetland Sheepdog varies, expect to spend at least $250. Potential show dogs may sell for $1,000 or more. Generally, a younger puppy will be less expensive than an older dog, because less time and money will have been invested in it.

Food may cost as much as $30 or $40 a month. You must also purchase equipment for feeding, grooming, and housing your dog. A dog requires annual immunizations against all infectious diseases as well as an annual heartworm test (when you live in an area where this disease is endemic; see page 46). Puppies and adult dogs may also have to be wormed. If you do not plan to breed your Sheltie, spaying or neutering is recommended. This will cost from

$75 to $150. If your dog should get sick or injured, it may need additional, sometimes costly, medical attention.

Finally, you will have to pay an annual licensing fee to your county or city. You will have to pay a fee to register your dog with the AKC as well as annual dues if you join the American Shetland Sheepdog Association.

The long-term expenses of owning a Shetland Sheepdog are much greater than the purchase price. Therefore, carefully consider these costs before you decide to buy a dog.

Bringing Your Puppy Home

Once you have selected the best puppy for you, you will have to arrange to take it home. The puppy should be seven weeks old when it moves to its new home. A puppy of this age should adapt very easily to its new environment but not be old enough to have picked up many bad habits. Recent studies have shown that during their eighth week, puppies become especially sensitive to environmental changes. If you cannot pick up the puppy during the seventh week, wait until the ninth week. Rather than risk creating behavior problems, wait until the puppy is ready for change.

If you select a Sheltie puppy from a local breeder, visit your puppy several times before bringing it home. This will allow your puppy to get used to you and can help alleviate some of the stress that a newly separated puppy experiences.

Indoor Requirements

I have previously mentioned that the diminutive size of the Shetland Sheepdog offers many advantages when it comes to indoor space requirements. Logic dictates that a smaller dog requires a smaller space, and in this case, that is true. However, dogs are territorial animals. Although a Sheltie's territory does not need to be very large, it must not be too small.

A Shetland Sheepdog, whether an adult or a puppy, requires a quiet living area where it can feel comfortable and secure. Inside your home, you must provide your dog with a territory of its own—its regular eating and sleeping areas. In locating these areas, keep in mind that once established, these areas should not be moved. The dog will feel secure and protected only if it has a quiet, reliable place to rest undisturbed. This area should neither isolate the dog nor subject it to heavy human traffic.

Good resting areas are in corners where the dog is protected on two sides. These areas should also be draft-free and not in direct sunlight. The area should also make confining the dog's movements easy when you go to bed or when you leave the house. Of equal importance is that the Sheltie's sleeping area be at the right temperature. A puppy requires the temperature

to be between 70 and 75°F (21–24°C). This range is warm enough to help prevent the puppy from catching colds and is not so warm as to make the dog sensitive to outside cold.

A Sheltie's sleeping area may be equipped with either a sleeping box and pad or a cage with a pad. Make this choice in advance, depending on your method of housebreaking. (See the chapter, Basic and Advanced Training, page 90). I recommend using a cage. It can also be invaluable for transporting and disciplining your puppy. Dogs are instinctively den animals. The confined space will make a puppy feel safer and more comfortable than would an open sleeping box.

The cage should be approximately 24 inches (61 cm) high by 24 inches (61 cm) wide by 30 inches (76 cm) long. It must have strong welds that cannot be broken by an active puppy.

The cage will be your puppy's house when you are not around to supervise. Some cages can also be used to carry your puppy when you go for a drive or to the veterinarian.

If you decide not to use a cage, purchase a sleeping box. Make sure it is large enough to accommodate a full-grown, spread-out dog. Line the box with cedar shavings and shredded newspapers. Then place an old blanket over this layer. Your dog will find this very comfortable for sleeping.

If you are purchasing a sleeping box, avoid those made of wicker or other soft wood

Be prepared for your new Sheltie puppy and buy supplies in advance.

materials. An active puppy can easily chew apart these types of beds. Likewise, if you decide to build your own box, use only non-splintering hardwoods. Because many stains and paints are toxic, leave the box unfinished.

When you are bringing home an unhousebroken puppy, do not give it an expensive pad. Puppies have little control over their bladder or bowels, so anything used in their bed should be either disposable or washable. In addition, be sure that anything you put into the bed is clean. Puppies are very susceptible to ailments because their immune system is not fully developed, and their resistance to disease is low.

Like its sleeping place, a dog's feeding place should never be changed. Changes in sleeping and feeding places can cause your pet unnecessary stress. An animal under stress may exhibit behavioral changes as well as changes in many biological functions, including problems with digestion and excretion. Placing your dog's feeding area into an easily cleaned room, such as the kitchen, is best.

Outdoor Requirements

Unlike most toy and miniature breeds, the Shetland Sheepdog is a rugged breed and may be kept outdoors—in most climates, all year round. However, bringing your Sheltie indoors on cold winter nights is advisable.

If you decide your dog is to live outdoors or if you leave your dog outside when you are not home, you must provide it with a fenced enclosure or run. The run should be at least 6 feet (2 m) wide by 15 feet (5 m) long by 6 feet (2 m) high. It should be constructed of strong chain-link fence. You can place partially buried boards around the bottom to prevent the dog

from digging under the fence. The run can be as large as your yard. However, it should not be smaller than the size stated.

Use a few inches of smooth stone as a base. This will provide drainage when it rains and prevent the dog from becoming muddy. Do not use concrete as a floor, because concrete will retain the smell of urine. The run must also provide your dog with some shade and shelter.

The best form of outdoor shelter is a doghouse. Whether you build your own or buy one, make sure it is raised several inches off the ground to avoid dampness and insects. The doghouse must be properly constructed to protect the dog against wind, rain, and cold, for even a minor draft can lead to serious respiratory ailments. The doghouse should be approximately 36 inches (91 cm) long, 30 inches (76 cm) high, and 30 inches (76 cm) wide. If the house is too small, the dog will not be able to stand or sleep comfortably. However, do not make the house too large. During cold weather, the dog's body will provide the only form of heat. For this reason, insulating the structure is also best.

Keeping your Sheltie's house as clean as possible is important. When constructing a doghouse, you can do several things to make cleaning easier. First, by hinging the roof, you can easily fold back the top of the doghouse to make the inside easily accessible. Next, you can line the floor of the structure with an easy-to-clean, waterproof material such as linoleum. You can also cover the linoleum with a thin layer of cedar shavings. Over that you can place an old blanket. The cedar shavings will serve several purposes. They will help absorb excess moisture that may get into the house. They will also make the floor more comfortable for sleeping. In addition, the natural oils in the

If your dog becomes injured and there is no muzzle available, you can use a necktie or a folded piece of cloth that is knotted in the center, tied under the chin, and knotted behind the neck. Tie this temporary muzzle firmly but not too tightly.

cedar shavings will help repel fleas from your dog and the doghouse.

To prevent the inside of the house from being exposed to the cold winter winds, you should place the front opening so that it faces south. If you hang a piece of canvas or a blanket over the opening, making sure it overlaps sufficiently, you can help eliminate drafts. If you live in a climate where winter nights become very cold, you should find a place indoors where your dog can sleep.

Additional Accessories

The first days after you bring your new puppy home are bound to be very busy and exciting. To avoid additional work or confusion, purchase the following items in advance, and keep them available.

The most important pieces of equipment, at least from your growing Sheltie's point of view, are the food and water dishes. Both food and water dishes should be nonbreakable, heavy, and sturdy enough so that a Sheltie with a voracious appetite cannot tip them over. Plastic, stainless steel, and ceramic are all suitable materials. If you choose to use a ceramic bowl, however, be sure it was not fired with a lead-based glaze. Using bowls covered with these glazes, over a long period of time, can cause lead poisoning.

During the life of your Sheltie, purchasing more than one collar may or may not be necessary. Your puppy will require a light collar but not necessarily a strong one. I recommend using either a leather or nylon collar that is adjustable to fit both a Sheltie puppy and adult. Bear in mind, though, that these collars deteriorate with age and would therefore need to be replaced eventually. If your Sheltie is an adult, you may choose to use a chain collar, but be sure it is not too heavy or bulky for your dog. Another type of collar that you may want to purchase is a choke-chain collar, which can come in very handy when it is time to teach your dog the basic commands.

Leashes come in a wide variety of lengths and materials. You may want to purchase more than one type. For regular walks, use a leash that is only a few feet long. This will enable you to bring the dog to your side quickly, should the need arise. It will also prevent your Sheltie from taking a destructive stroll through

Toys are an important part of a Sheltie's life, regardless of their age. Make sure that toys are of a suitable size so they cannot be swallowed.

Playtime is important to both you and your Sheltie because it strengthens the bond between you and helps relieve stress; be sure to take the time to enjoy each other's company.

Shelties are a friendly breed. Under the right conditions, they get along well with other dogs as well as with other types of pets.

Shelties love to run in open spaces.

Spend quality time with your dogs.

your neighbor's perfectly manicured garden. If you are lucky enough to possess a large yard, a 30-foot (10-m) leash with an automatic reel is useful. Because a Sheltie is not a large, strong dog, you do not need to get a leash made of anything stronger than leather or nylon. This is doubly true of Sheltie puppies. Sheltie puppies will chew, or attempt to chew, on anything that passes in front of their noses. Therefore, you should never purchase a chain leash for your puppy. Chewing on the chain can damage a puppy's teeth.

A good safety device that you may want to purchase is reflecting tags or tape. The tags or tape attach to your dog's collar and leash, making both dog and owner more visible at night when headlights shine on them. This will make your nighttime walks much safer. You should also attach an identity tag, with your address and phone number, to the dog's collar, This simple and inexpensive precaution could prove to be invaluable should your Sheltie ever become lost.

The owners of Shetland Sheepdogs rarely need a muzzle for their dogs. However, you should keep one readily available just in case. If you are planning on taking your Sheltie abroad, note that some foreign countries require all dogs to wear muzzles. A muzzle may also be necessary if your dog becomes seriously hurt and has to be taken to a veterinarian. A dog in severe pain may react unpredictably, so be prepared. When buying a muzzle, get one that can be adjusted for size. Remember that the head of a Sheltie puppy and that of an adult dog are very different.

Flea sprays, tweezers, and rubbing alcohol are helpful in case of external parasites. Flea sprays come in many forms, including aerosols, pump-on liquids, and alcohol-based liquids that you can rub on. Flea-control products also come in other forms such as foggers, powders, dips, and collars. Use tweezers to remove ticks properly and rubbing alcohol to disinfect the wound.

Dog Toys

As with children, toys are an essential part of a dog's life and are important to both its physical and mental well-being. Toys signify playtime. They let your puppy know that there is more to life than training sessions, eating, and sleeping. Playing with toys gives a dog exercise and allows a dog to work out frustration that it may be experiencing. In addition, toys allow a puppy to develop its survival instincts. If you watch your Sheltie playing with its toys, you will see this for yourself. Watch your puppy get low to the ground and attempt to creep up on its target. Observe it studying its opponent, waiting until the time is right. Then watch it pounce and render its prey harmless. This entire act may take all of five seconds, but it is part of every puppy's instincts to survive. If all this is not enough to convince you of the importance of toys, I will give you one last reason to use them. Giving your puppy toys will spare your furniture, clothing, and other valued possessions from small, but well-defined, teeth marks.

From the time a puppy begins to teethe, it should always have a chewable toy on which to gnaw. Rawhide bones are excellent chew toys. They become soft enough to not harm a young puppy's teeth and, at the same time, will help strengthen your Sheltie's jaw muscles. Since a Sheltie puppy can quickly reduce a small rawhide bone to almost nothing, make sure to replace the bone before it becomes small enough for the puppy to swallow whole. Avoid giving your dog any toy that it can shred and swallow, for this can cause choking or blockage of the digestive tract.

When choosing toys for your Sheltie, make sure they are designed for small dogs and are made of 100 percent nontoxic materials. Some forms of plastic are toxic, and many forms of wood can splinter. To be on the safe side, never give your Sheltie any painted items. Some older types of paint contain lead, which may be harmful if swallowed in excess. Varnished toys are also potentially toxic and should be avoided.

Not all your Sheltie's toys need be store bought. Some of the best times my dogs have ever had were when we played hide and seek with some big cardboard boxes or shopping bags. Tennis balls are also among their favorite toys. If you decide to use a ball from around

your house, it should be of the proper size and material. Do not use golf balls or Ping-Pong balls, because they can be chewed on and swallowed. Do not be afraid to use your imagination. You can use many simple household items to keep your puppy entertained for hours.

Just remember to be selective in the items you give your puppy for toys. A Sheltie puppy will chew almost anything that will fit into its mouth. In addition, a mischievous Sheltie will tend to seek out anything with your scent, such as your old shoes and clothing. For this reason, keep these items out of your puppy's reach. Also, never give your puppy either your old slippers or toys that resemble valuable objects. A Sheltie puppy does not know the difference between an old slipper and your new one. This is true of anything of value to you—letters, money, keys, and so on. Keep all valuable items away from your puppy, and you will prevent it from developing bad habits.

CARING FOR YOUR SHELTIE

Necessary Preparations

The first few days after a puppy is brought into its new home are usually hectic. Preparing yourself and your house before bringing your puppy home is therefore a good idea. By taking a few steps in advance, you can greatly reduce the confusion when you bring your puppy home.

Purchase beforehand all the necessary equipment and accessories, such as food and water dishes, collars, leashes, grooming supplies, and so on. In addition, you should also choose the puppy's food (as recommended by the breeder) and purchase an adequate supply of it.

When you have bought all the supplies and have placed them in readily accessible locations, begin to puppy-proof your home. Remember that a young puppy is very curious. As it roams through your house, it will sniff, paw at, and chew almost everything. For this reason, place all potential hazards out of the puppy's reach.

Remove all poisons, including paints, cleaners, disinfectants, insecticides, and antifreeze. Store them in an area inaccessible to your puppy. Also, remove all sharp objects such as broken glass, nails, and staples. If you have an older home, make sure your dog does not eat paint chips containing lead.

Make sure you give your Sheltie time to adjust to its new environment.

Electric wires must also be moved out of your puppy's reach. A dog chewing on electric wires can be injured or killed by the resulting shock.

Finally, you should decide where the Sheltie's feeding and sleeping areas will be, and equip them accordingly. By doing all of these things, you can make the upcoming transition period much easier for both you and your puppy.

Adjustment

Most people find it difficult to adjust to a new environment. We undergo some emotional stress when we change jobs and are introduced to our new workmates or when we move and meet the new neighbors. We feel loneliness because we miss friends and loved ones. We are uncertain of what the future holds in this new place. We miss the security of everything we left behind.

A young puppy has much the same feelings the first days when it is home with you. You are taking it from the security of its mother and siblings and placing it into an unfamiliar world full of strange new sights and sounds. The stress of this move makes your puppy's first few hours in your home very important. You now have an emotionally insecure and very impressionable seven-week-old puppy in your home. You must make the transition period go as smoothly as possible. You must let your puppy know it is entering a calm, safe, and

CHECKLIST

Puppy Safety Rules

Before bringing your Sheltie puppy home, review these seven rules with your family and friends. In addition to preventing injury, these rules will help your puppy to feel comfortable and safe in its new home and increase its confidence in you and your family.

1 Avoid unnecessary excitement. New owners have a tendency to invite over everyone they know to see the new member of their family. Young visitors will usually run around screaming with excitement. Let the puppy adjust to its new surroundings in peace before subjecting it to numerous strangers.

2 Prohibit rough play. Puppies are very fragile creatures and should be handled with care. Avoid overhandling. Make sure the children do not poke the puppy, pull its ears, or subject it to any other rough handling.

3 Be sure everyone in your household knows the proper way to lift and carry your puppy (see page 24 for technique).

If any visitors desire to pick up the puppy, instruct them how to do so.

4 Avoid picking up the puppy too much. Allow it to do its own walking whenever possible. This will provide some exercise and improve the puppy's motor skills and physical abilities.

5 Do not give bones or other hard objects to a young puppy. Until a puppy reaches about six months of age, it has only its milk teeth and cannot chew hard objects such as meat bones.

6 Do not subject your puppy to unnecessary heights. Avoid placing it onto tables, counters, or beds, because a fall could be disastrous. When placing the puppy onto an elevated surface, such as a grooming table, someone must be present the entire time to assure the puppy's safety.

7 Try never to leave the puppy unsupervised during the first few weeks.

secure home. Assure your puppy that it need not fear and you will take care of it. Make your puppy's first day home a quiet one.

When your puppy arrives, it will probably want to urinate or defecate. Instead of entering your house, walk the puppy to a place you have chosen for its elimination area. Give the puppy about ten minutes to relieve itself, and then praise and pet it for doing so. This will help the puppy learn to defecate and urinate outdoors.

To help the puppy adjust, let it sniff around your home undisturbed. Then help it learn the

When lifting your puppy, place one hand under the puppy's hindquarters while supporting the abdomen and chest with the other.

location of its food and water dishes. Let your puppy continue to roam about, but do feel free to pet it and play with it. When it tires, pick it up and put it into its sleeping box or cage. Within a few days, the puppy should learn where its sleeping area is and when tired, find its bed on its own.

To me, the next step in training your puppy is the hardest test you will face. Furthermore, it is your first test. Failure here will mean greater problems in the future. Your puppy will probably whine, whimper, and wail because it is in an unfamiliar place and because it misses its mother and siblings. However, you must remain firm. If the puppy sleeps in a cage, do not let it out. If you do, it will wail every time it wants to leave the cage. If you use a sleeping box, you might try to reassure the puppy by speaking softly, but do not take it from the box. Your puppy must learn to deal with loneliness as soon as possible.

By the time it is eight weeks old, a puppy should be fully weaned and eating from a dish. When feeding your puppy, you should follow a few fundamental rules. First, be sure to feed your puppy the same kind of food used by the breeder. Changes in surroundings will cause the puppy a certain amount of stress, which may affect its digestive system. By not changing its diet, you will avoid digestive problems. Second, try to feed your puppy on the same schedule used by the breeder. However, if that schedule is inconvenient, change the feeding times slowly to meet your schedule. Finally, never

bother your dog while it is eating (or sleeping). A dog that is surprised may sometimes act unpredictably. Be sure also to explain this rule to your children.

If you must leave the house during your puppy's first few days, be sure it is not left alone. If no family member is available, ask a neighbor or a close friend to puppy-sit. An unsupervised, curious puppy means only one thing—a mess.

Soon after your puppy arrives, you must begin to train it. Training will require time, energy, patience, understanding, and of course, love. From the minute your Sheltie arrives, begin to teach it its name. (Other essential lessons are described in detail in the Basic and Advanced Training chapter, page 77.) Remember, the longer you wait to begin training, the harder it will be for your dog to learn.

Handling a Sheltie

Everyone in your family must learn how to lift and carry your puppy. Improper handling can pain and possibly injure the dog. Place one hand under the puppy's chest, and support the rear and hind legs with the other hand. Never pick up the puppy by placing only one hand under its abdomen. Never pick it up by the scruff of the neck. Both of these methods can hurt the puppy.

A healthy, adult Sheltie will weigh only 14 to 16 pounds (6.4–7.7 kg), so most people can lift it in the same fashion as a puppy. I do urge you to pick up and carry an adult dog only when necessary. If your Sheltie can jump over an obstacle or climb up a flight of stairs to its destination, then let it. A herding dog needs a lot of exercise.

When moving an injured dog, take special precautions. If possible, wait for an experienced person to lift and carry the dog. If you must do this yourself, first place a muzzle onto the dog. A dog in pain may act unpredictably and snap at anyone who tries to help it. Then place one arm between the dog's forepaws. The hand on this arm should support the dog's midsection while the forearm should support the dog's head. Use the other hand to support the dog's rear and hind legs. Do not allow the dog's midsection to sag or its head to fall forward. (For further information on treating a sick dog, consult the Ailments and Illnesses chapter, page 55.)

Shelties and Children

The Shetland Sheepdog is a herding breed. When it is with children, many of its inbred personality traits become even more evident. Shelties are loyal dogs and are full of pep and spirit. They will joyfully play with children while, at the same time, be alert for any signs of danger. This breed is rarely the aggressor in any confrontation. However, if any member of its family were attacked, the Sheltie would defend that person with a ferocity that belies its small size. Shelties are small, but they are quick to think and maneuver. In addition, their self-assurance and ruggedness make them formidable opponents, even to very large dogs.

A special bond will form between a Sheltie and the children in its family. Many years of hard life on the Shetland Islands have impressed upon this breed the need to cling to one family, be loyal, and obey its commands.

Although the Sheltie is a hardy and rugged breed, their small bodies will not stand up to all the abuse that many children can dish out. Even the most loyal of Shelties may turn and nip at a child (or adult) it feels is deliberately trying to

Don't disturb your puppy while it is eating.

Dogs are pack animals that establish a social ranking.

hurt it. All animals, including humans, have this instinctive defensive reaction. Children should be taught not to pinch and pull on the dog's hair, tail, or ears and always to avoid going near the dog's eyes. Children should be taught never to disturb a Sheltie while it is eating or sleeping. Explain that although the dog is a loving pet, it may nip at them if surprised or frightened. Also teach your children how to meet a strange dog. They should not go to the dog but, instead, let it approach them. They should not move suddenly, and they should keep their hands below the dog's head. If the dog sniffs their hands and is still friendly, the children can pet it.

You can help assure an enduring relationship between your children and your Sheltie by involving them in the responsibilities of dog care. Encourage your children to help feed, groom, and walk your dog.

Shelties and the New Baby

Reports of attacks on infants by family dogs lead many people to get rid of their devoted pets when they have a new baby. This is truly a shame, for Shelties are at their best when they have children—including infants—to love. If you have or are planning to have a baby, take heart. Animal behavior experts who have studied this problem thoroughly have concluded that most dogs will not be aggressive toward a baby. They also believe, however, that dogs that tend to chase and kill small animals, or those that are aggressive toward people in general, should never be left unsupervised with an infant.

You should take several precautions to assure your Sheltie's acceptance of your new baby. Before the baby's birth, train your dog to sit or lie down for long periods of time. As you increase the length of time the dog remains still, accustom it to other activities occurring around it at the same time. Reward your dog if it stays still and does not attempt to follow you.

Once training is complete, simulate the other activities that will occur after the baby arrives. Use a doll to imitate carrying, feeding, changing, and bathing the newborn.

After the birth of the infant, give the dog something the baby used in the hospital in order for it to sniff, smell, and become accustomed to the baby's scent. Upon returning home from the hospital, allow the mother to greet the dog without the baby. Then place the baby into the nursery, and deny the dog access by using a screen door or folding gate. In this way, the dog can see and hear the infant and get used to its presence before dog and baby actually meet.

When you finally introduce the dog and baby, one person should control and reward the dog while another person holds the baby. Have the dog sit, and then show it to the baby. Keep them together for as long as the dog remains calm. For the next week or two, gradually increase the length of the dog's visit.

Never allow your dog to wander unsupervised in the presence of an infant. However, be sure to allow your dog to be present during activities that involve your newborn. Do not let the dog feel neglected because of the infant. The more activities in which you allow the dog to participate, the stronger the bond will be between Sheltie and child.

Shelties and Other Pets

Shetland Sheepdogs should get along well with other pets. Your Sheltie will rarely show signs of jealousy as long as it receives sufficient attention. If the pets substantially differ in size, such as with birds, hamsters, gerbils, and so on, not allowing these animals to play freely with your Sheltie is best.

If you own two Shelties, you will rarely have any problems. In fact, the dogs will probably enjoy each other's companionship. Many members of the herding breeds work in tandem with other dogs, and the Sheltie is no exception. You must remember, however, not to give the older dog any less attention than previously. Show the older dog that you care for it as much as always, then leave the two to establish their own relationship. You should have little difficulty getting the two dogs to live in harmony. In fact, if you show no favoritism to either dog, the older one should adopt and protect the younger one.

Before buying a second dog, however, remember that you will need additional equipment, including separate sleeping boxes or cages and food dishes. Also be sure you have the extra time, space, and money that a second dog requires.

Canine Social Behavior

If you plan to own more than one Sheltie, or if you wish to understand why dogs react as they do to humans and to each other, you must examine the dog's instinctive nature. Canine social behavior is similar to that of wild wolves. Wolves are pack hunting animals and require companionship. This is also true for Shelties, though humans can thoroughly satisfy their need for company. Because of this need, you can punish a dog by isolating it during training sessions. In addition, as pack animals, dogs develop among themselves a dominant–subordinate relationship. This relationship allows a stable existence between dogs. Thus, if one of your dogs tends to be more dominant than another, do not worry. This occurs naturally and will prevent fights between dogs for food, living space, and human attention. This social ranking is largely determined by size, age, strength, and sex. This social dominance also allows a dog to obey its owner. During training, a dog learns that it is subordinate to the human members of the household.

Both dogs and wolves mark their frequently traveled paths or territory by urinating, defecating, and scratching the ground. In addition to such boundary marking, females secrete a scent that signals their being in heat.

Female Dogs

If you own a female Shetland Sheepdog, you must take special precautions regarding pregnancy. A Sheltie female normally comes into estrus (in heat or in season) twice a year. Estrus is the period during which the female accepts mating with the male. This period usually lasts four to fourteen days. (If you choose to breed your female, refer to the Breeding Shelties chapter, page 57.) If you choose not to breed your female, you can take several measures to prevent pregnancy. As stated earlier, if you plan never to breed the female, have her spayed. The benefits are numerous.

Spaying your female dog will prevent her from roaming away from your home when she is in season. Also, it is the only sure way to prevent an unwanted litter. Finally, an unspayed female may suffer many ailments that a spayed dog can avoid. These include false pregnancies, uterine infections, ovarian cysts, and many types of tumors that attack the reproductive system.

Because spaying a dog is permanent, you must be positive that you will never want to breed your female. If you are at all in doubt, do not have your dog spayed. As your female gets older, you may wish to continue the line of the dog you have grown to love over the years. You can attempt to do this by breeding your female with another purebred male Sheltie. You cannot do this with a spayed dog. If you decide not to spay, there are other ways to avoid pregnancy in your female dog.

The most obvious way is to keep your female away from all male dogs. This may not be as easy as it sounds. You would be amazed at the distances a male dog will travel to find a female in heat. In addition, stray male dogs may camp outside your house, waiting for you to drop your guard. For this reason, you must never let your female go outside alone during estrus. Even if you have a fenced-in yard, she would not be safe. To get at a female in heat, male dogs can perform supercanine feats.

During her season, your female will also undergo some attitude changes. The mating urge is very great at this time. Your female may be less obedient to your commands, especially if a male is nearby. So always walk your female on a leash when she is in heat, or you may end up running after her as she ignores your pleas for her to return.

You can consult your veterinarian about additional precautions. Many show dog owners have their veterinarian administer estrus-control medication. In this way, they can show their females without the worry of upsetting the male competition. This drug, however, may have side effects. Chlorophyll tablets are also available through your veterinarian. These tablets help neutralize the odor of the female's secretions.

For a female to discharge small amounts of blood during her season is perfectly natural. To prevent staining your rugs or furniture, you may wish to confine her to an easy-to-clean room. Sanitary napkins and diapers are also available for dogs in heat.

Boarding Your Sheltie

During the course of your lives together, almost inevitably you and your Sheltie will have to spend a prolonged period away from each other. You may be suddenly called away from home or have to go on a business trip, or maybe you need a vacation. If you live alone or if the other members of your family are going to join you, you must arrange to have someone look after your dog.

Having a dependable neighbor whom the dog knows and trusts and whom you can instruct about your Sheltie's eating, playing, and walking routine is ideal. In this way, your dog will be able to stay in its familiar environment, your home. Unfortunately, things do not always work out this easily.

If you must board your Sheltie, start by contacting the breeder from whom you purchased it. If the breeder is willing to care for your dog, you can be assured of expert care for a Shetland Sheepdog. If this is not possible, you may decide to place dog the dog into a boarding kennel.

Before you leave your Sheltie at a boarding kennel, I recommend that you inspect the facilities thoroughly. Make sure that the sleeping areas and runs are clean and that the operating staff at the kennel are knowledgeable. If all the conditions at the boarding facility are suitable to you, there need be little worry about your dog. A mature Shetland Sheepdog will have little problem adjusting to this new

environment. If it can be avoided, however, you should never leave a puppy younger than six months old, either alone or at a boarding kennel, for a long period of time.

Vacation Time

Vacationing with your Sheltie can be fun for both of you, but it takes planning. If you plan to travel by air, you will be happy to know that all major airlines will make arrangements to transport your dog. The airline can supply a travel crate and have pressurized cabins where they can house your dog during the flight. Before the flight, take your dog for a long walk, and allow it to eliminate. It is also good to feed your dog several hours before flying. This will minimize travel sickness. The cost and rules of pet transport service vary from airline to airline, so be sure to check the details ahead of time.

If you decide to vacation in a foreign country, obtaining from the appropriate consulate a copy of the country's law pertaining to dogs is advisable. While most countries have minimal regulations about dogs, some do require quarantine. Some countries have laws about the use of muzzles. Most countries do require that your dog be immunized against the major infectious diseases. You will need a valid health certificate from a licensed veterinarian. If you should require veterinary service while you are abroad, you can get helpful information from the American consulate or embassy.

If you decide to vacation in the United States you may choose to travel by railroad. Like the airlines, all major railroads will transport dogs. Dogs are usually kept in shipping crates in the baggage car. You can check with

The Sheltie's small size makes it easy to bring them just about anywhere, including a trip to the park.

the railroad company to see if they will supply the crate.

Traveling by car can be the most fun for your dog. Many Shelties actually seem to enjoy car travel and will spend hours watching the passing scenery. When traveling by automobile, do not allow your pet to have free run of the car. You should confine your Sheltie to either its cage or the back seat. Open the window enough to give it some fresh air, but do not expose it to a draft. Drafts can cause eye, ear, and throat problems. Make rest stops at least every two hours, and allow the dog to walk and relieve itself. Keep it on a leash so that it will not run away. The inside of a car can get very hot, so allow your dog to drink regularly.

Many young dogs may get carsick if they are not used to traveling. As a precaution, you can obtain motion sickness tablets from your veterinarian.

Once you have made all your traveling arrangements, it is time to pack. Your sheepdog suitcase should contain the following: food and water dishes, collar, leash, brush, blanket (and cage), and muzzle. Bringing enough canned or dry food to last the entire trip is advisable. If you normally feed your Sheltie fresh foods, accustom it to canned or dry food for a few weeks before your departure.

HOW-TO: GROOMING

Your Sheltie will need a thorough brushing every day and periodic grooming to maintain its coat in prime condition. Start handling and grooming your puppy as soon as possible so it will become accustomed to the procedure.

Equipment

Every Sheltie owner should have the following supplies: a comb, a slicker brush, a stiff-bristle brush, scissors, nail clippers, tweezers, ear-cleaning solution, and cotton swabs. Because the Sheltie is a relatively small dog and grooming it is easier when the dog is at table level, you may also want to consider purchasing a grooming table. No matter how experienced you become at grooming your Sheltie, you should always have a small bottle of styptic powder in case of accidents that result in bleeding.

Daily Brushing

Start by using the stiff-bristle brush, followed by a slicker brush on the dog's back and sides, avoiding all the areas of the body with longer hair. By using the bristle-brush first, you can untangle snarls before removing any shedding undercoat with the slicker brush. Use the stiff-bristle brush on the feathered hair on the legs, abdomen, chest, and tail. Once brushing is complete, use a comb to remove all loose hairs. If the feathered hairs of your Sheltie become too long, you can trim them using sharp scissors. When brushing your Sheltie, you should look for signs of flea infestations. If you notice any other skin condition, seek the advice of your veterinarian.

Tipping the Ears

The shape of a Sheltie's ears may vary somewhat, resulting in differences as to how they should be groomed. When a Sheltie assumes an attentive position, its ears should stand semi-erect, with just the tips folding forward. Unfortunately, most Shelties need assistance to obtain this look. If your Sheltie has low, hound-like ears, you can trim off all the excess hair around the tips in order to reduce the weight that pulls them down. If your dog does not have bent tips, then you may want to weight (or tape) them down. Consult with a breeder, veterinarian, or groomer about the best weighting procedure.

Ear and Eye Care

To avoid infections, trim all excess hair from the ear canals. A pair of tweezers helps remove any loose hairs that have gotten into the ear. Carefully remove any wax build-up using a commercial ear-cleaning solution. To clean the ear, hold it open with one hand, and gently clean inside the outer ear with a cotton ball dipped into cleaning solution. Use a fresh cotton ball for each ear. You can clean the outermost portions of the ear canal using a cotton swab that has been dipped into the solution.

Inspect your Sheltie's eyes regularly as well. Be sure they are clear and free of any discharge. You can clean around your dog's eyes with a moistened cotton ball to remove any dirt. Again, use a fresh cotton ball for each eye. If you notice any damage or inflammation, contact your veterinarian for advice.

Caution: Before cleaning your dog's eyes and ears for the first time, consult with your veterinarian to learn the proper methods.

Nail and Paw Care

Check the bottoms of the dog's paws, and trim the hair between the paws as short as possible. This will improve the dog's traction and reduce the chance of infection in wet weather. Before you trim your dog's nails, learn how to use a pair of clippers. An experi-

You should regularly check your Sheltie's teeth for tartar build-up.

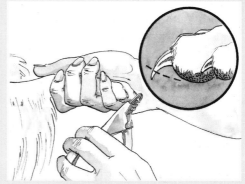

When trimming your Sheltie's nails, be sure to clip them at an angle and do not cut the pink area called the quick.

enced groomer or veterinarian can show you how to use them.

The center of the dog's nail is called the quick and contains the blood vessels and nerve endings. If you cut the quick, you will cause the dog much pain. Always cut the nail as close to the quick as possible, and be sure to hold your pet's paw firmly but gently. Be sure to have the styptic powder on hand.

Tooth Care

Tooth care begins with feeding your Sheltie plenty of hard foods to prevent the buildup of tartar. Excessive tartar can lead to deteriorating gums and tooth loss. You should also brush your dog's teeth once a week with a commercial toothpaste specifically for dogs. Before brushing, check the dog's teeth and gums for signs of infection and tartar buildup. Your veterinarian can scrape off excessive tartar.

Bathing

Bathing should be thought of as a last resort. Shampooing your Sheltie can remove the natural oils that weatherproof the coat. Excessive bathing also tends to dry out your Sheltie's skin and promote excessive shedding. Try to clean your dog with a wet, slightly soapy cloth.

When bathing is necessary, use a shampoo formulated for dogs. Be sure to rinse out all of the shampoo, which may irritate the dog's skin. Dry your Sheltie by rubbing it briskly with a towel. (You can also use a blow dryer.) Once most of the water has been removed, brush and comb out the coat. Keep your dog indoors and away from drafts while it dries.

NUTRITION

Understanding Nutrition

The nutritional requirements of dogs have probably changed little since they were first trained to perform domestic work. What has changed, however, is our understanding of animal nutrition and our ability to utilize our knowledge to provide our pets with more healthy foods.

All foods are composed of one or several nutrient groups—proteins, fats, carbohydrates, vitamins, minerals, trace elements, and water. These nutrients are essential for the proper growth and metabolism of a dog. By supplying these nutrients in the correct proportions, you can create a well-balanced diet and ensure your dog's proper nutrition.

The type and quantity of nutrients a dog needs depends on several factors. Individual growth rate, the kind of work the dog does, exercise, metabolic rate, and many environmental factors all influence the quantity of food your dog requires. For instance, a Shetland Sheepdog that spends its days in the hot fields herding sheep requires a higher-energy diet than does a Sheltie that spends most of its day confined to a house.

Age is another factor that influences your Sheltie's nutritional requirements. The amount of food a dog needs changes as it gets older.

Feed your Sheltie a high-quality diet to ensure proper nutrition throughout its life.

As a result, a dog may become overweight or underweight if its body requirements have changed but its diet has not. For this reason, you must watch your dog's weight and increase or decrease its food intake when necessary.

Nutritional Needs

The National Research Council (NRC), a division of the National Academy of Science of the United States, has compiled and interpreted vast quantities of data. It has published this data in an almost complete study entitled "Nutrient Requirements of Dogs." This report establishes the minimum amount of each nutrient needed to maintain the health of the average adult dog as well as the requirements for growing puppies.

This study is utilized by practically every company that manufactures commercial dog food to help formulate their products. In fact, in order for a dog food to be certified as complete in the United States, it must meet or exceed all of the nutritional requirements established by the NRC and must pass actual feeding tests on dogs.

Scientifically, dogs are classified as carnivores, that is, meat eaters. They have the ability, however, to utilize a remarkably wide variety of foodstuffs to meet their nutritional needs. Thus, if you were reading the labels on several brands of dog food, you might notice

The Basic Nutrient Groups

Nutrient (Sources)	Nutritional Value and Symptoms of Deficiencies
Proteins (meat, eggs, fish, milk, soybean meal, brewer's yeast, wheat germ)	Provide amino acids essential for growth, development, and maintenance of strong bones and muscles; promote production of antibodies, enzymes, and hormones; deficiencies include poor growth, weight loss, loss of appetite, and poor hair and coat.
Fats (meat, vegetable oils)	Provide a source of energy and heat; supply essential fatty acids and fat-soluble vitamins (A, D, E, and K); make food more palatable; necessary for proper development of skin and coat; deficiencies include dry and coarse coat and skin lesions.
Carbohydrates (sugars, starches)	Help regulate energy balance; supply fiber and roughage to help regulate digestive system and help prevent diarrhea/constipation.
Vitamins (brewer's yeast, vegetables, fruits, cod liver oil, wheat germ oil)	Important in preventing numerous illnesses and diseases; help in regulating many bodily functions including growth and fertility.
Minerals/Trace Minerals (bones, meat, grains, fruit, vegetables)	Important in preventing numerous ailments and diseases; help in regulating many bodily functions including bone formation; help regulate water balance within a dog's body. (Trace minerals are so named because they are required in very small quantities.)

many differences. Therefore, determining which food is best for your dog is very difficult. To help you decide, I recommend that you seek the advice of your breeder and your veterinarian. Your breeder will know what worked best for your dog's dam (mother) as well as for other Shelties. Your veterinarian will have a working knowledge of dog foods based on the experiences of other clients. A veterinarian will also be able to recommend a special diet should your Sheltie's health dictate the need for one.

As you can probably guess by now, I strongly urge all dog owners to use a high-quality commercial dog food. When trying to prepare a dog's food from scratch, giving your pet either too much or too little of an essential nutrient becomes all too easy. This process is also much more expensive and significantly more time consuming.

Types of Commercial Dog Food

Dry dog foods: These are by far the most popular type of dog food. They can be pellets, kibbles, extruded shapes, or whole biscuits. As the name implies, dry foods are low in moisture content (usually about 10 to 12 percent). They contain mostly grains, cereal by-products, animal and soybean meals, and fats as well as vitamin and mineral supplements.

Semimoist dog foods: These foods are moderate in moisture content (between 25 and 30 percent). They contain much the same ingredients as dry foods but usually with less meat meal and more whole meat. Semimoist foods are usually formed into patties or simulated meat chunks.

Canned dog foods: These foods are usually very high in moisture (sometimes as much as 75 percent). Some canned foods are nutritionally complete, while others are made to add to dry foods to make them more palatable. Thus, when you buy canned dog foods, you should be extra careful in your selection.

Note: When buying commercial dog foods, be sure to read the labels carefully for nutritional information and feeding tips.

Special foods: Advances in animal health research have led to the development of commercial dog foods designed to supply complete nutrition during every phase of your dog's life. In addition to puppy foods, you can find special diets for active dogs, inactive dogs, overweight dogs, and older dogs. Some companies even make special diets for dogs with medical problems such as heart conditions and kidney disorders. (These special medical diets are available only from your veterinarian.)

Food for the finicky eater: In general, Shetland Sheepdogs are not finicky eaters. On occasion, however, a Sheltie may not want to eat the food that the breeder or veterinarian recommends. If you happen to own such a Sheltie and you are using a dry dog food, you might try adding some canned all-meat dog food to the diet. If this does not work, you may have to try several types of food before you find one your dog will eat.

Table Scraps

Many people feel that they must give their precious pooches a sampling from their own nightly banquet. Be warned that this practice has great potential for teaching your Sheltie some bad habits, such as begging. In addition, many foods may be harmful to your dog. If you do feel that your dog's devotion has earned it a special reward, then be sure that you give it the right type of scraps.

Avoid giving your Sheltie any undercooked meat, particularly pork (which can carry a parasite that can cause trichinosis) and chicken (which can carry harmful bacteria). Never feed your Sheltie any chicken that has the bones in it. Chicken bones splinter when they break, and a Sheltie can become injured if it swallows any

TIP

Diet

Dogs do not require a wide variety of foods and will not tire of eating the same thing every day. If you feed your Sheltie a high-quality, well-balanced diet, it can thrive on this food for its entire life. While I am not trying to imply that giving your dog a variety of high-quality commercial diets is bad, I do wish to point out that loss of appetite indicates a problem. If your dog is not eating properly, something is wrong either physically or emotionally. It may not be anything more than a mild stomach upset; however, if your Sheltie falls off its diet for two or three days, take it to your veterinarian.

(above) This Sheltie is taking some time out to get a drink of water. Always remember to have a fresh supply of water available for your dog to prevent dehydration, especially following exercise routines.

(right) Coat condition is a good indicator of whether your dog is receiving a balanced diet. This Sheltie's coat is in prime condition.

It is important to watch your Sheltie's weight and change its diet accordingly to prevent obesity.

sharp pieces. If you must feed your dog a real meat bone (even though dog biscuits and rawhide bones make excellent substitutes), then make sure it is a good, solid, well-cooked beef or pork bone.

Burying Food

Some dogs have a strong hereditary urge to bury bones or other foods for use during times of need. Do not be surprised if your Sheltie expresses a desire to bury a bone in the backyard. Of course, if the desire is strong enough and you prevent your dog from taking food outside, any Sheltie worth its salt will find another place to hide the food—perhaps under a piece of furniture, in with a potted plant, or even in the corner of a dark closet.

Because old food can build up quite an odor, I suggest that you allow a dog that shows a strong desire to hoard food to bury the occasional bone in the yard. This is better than having your Sheltie resurrect an old meal during a special dinner party.

Importance of Water

Of all the nutrients in a high-quality diet, none is more important than water. Water is vital to every living cell and comprises nearly 60 percent of your Sheltie's body weight. Unlike some other animals, dogs cannot store much water and need to replenish constantly whatever they lose. You must, therefore, always provide your dog with an adequate supply.

Your Sheltie's water intake will depend on several factors, including the air temperature, the type of food the dog eats, the amount of exercise it gets, and its temperament. Always having a fresh supply of clean water available to the dog so that it can drink as soon as it feels the need is best. Whenever you change your dog's water, be sure that the water is not too cold, especially after strenuous exercise, because it may cause cramping of the stomach muscles.

Special Considerations

While the NRC study provides the minimum requirements for growing and adult dogs, several additional factors may affect the type and quantity of nutrients that an individual animal may need. As I have stated earlier, exercise, metabolic rate, individual growth rates, the kind of work performed, and many environmental factors influence the quantity of food your dog requires.

In general, as a dog becomes older and less active, it needs less food (or at least fewer calories). An older dog can become overweight if its requirements have changed but its diet has not. You should therefore watch your dog's weight and change its food intake when necessary.

Coat condition is another good indicator of the adequacy of your Sheltie's diet. A dry coat and flaky skin may indicate a fat, fatty acid, or vitamin deficiency. This condition is often accompanied by scratching and is sometimes misdiagnosed by the owner as external parasites or other skin ailments. The proper diet should produce a soft and shiny coat, which is rich in color.

Shelties that receive a lot of exercise, are used for herding, or perform in field and Obedience trials will usually require a diet higher in calories. The same is true for dogs that spend a lot of time outdoors in cold weather. They may need as much as 50 percent more calories than their counterparts in warm climates. Once again, body weight and coat condition are the best indicators of how well your dog's diet meets its needs.

If for any reason you suspect that your dog's diet is not providing adequate nourishment, you should seek the advice of your veterinarian. A change in the diet may be needed, or a medical problem may need attention.

Proper nourishment is essential for your Sheltie's health.

Understanding Symptoms

Abnormal symptoms indicate that your dog is not well and that medical treatment may be necessary. A single abnormal symptom, or a combination of them, does not always point to a specific illness. The training of a veterinarian is usually needed to discover the cause of the problem.

Watch for loss of or excessive appetite or thirst, physical exhaustion, poor coat condition, excessive coughing or sneezing, frequent wheezing or running nose, repeated vomiting, pale gums, foul breath, slight paralysis or limping, trembling or shaking, sudden weight loss, any swelling or lumps on the body, cloudy or orange-colored urine, inability to urinate or uncontrollable urge to urinate, diarrhea, moaning or whimpering, a discharge from the eyes, and any unusual slobbering or salivation. If you notice any one or a combination of these symptoms, contact your veterinarian. Many diseases can cause severe damage if not treated promptly.

Two of the most common abnormal symptoms are vomiting and diarrhea. They occur frequently in dogs and do not always indicate a serious ailment. Therefore, they warrant further discussion.

Vomiting

Vomiting does not always indicate a problem. A mother with newborn puppies may

Preventive health care should begin early in your dog's life.

instinctively regurgitate food in an attempt to feed her pups. In addition, young dogs, especially puppies, often attack their food so greedily that their natural defense mechanisms send the food back up again. This behavior disappears as they mature. Nervous dogs may also vomit whenever something bothers them.

Vomiting also can be caused by internal parasites, an infection, numerous digestive ailments, and other diseases. Vomiting is usually accompanied by irregular bowel movements such as diarrhea. A dog with these symptoms needs veterinary attention.

Diarrhea

An occasional soft stool need not worry you, although diarrhea may follow. Continued watery bowel movements, however, indicate a serious ailment. Diarrhea, like vomiting, is a symptom of nearly every canine ailment, including distemper, worms, poisoning, nervous disorders, parvovirus, and intestinal blockages.

If diarrhea occurs infrequently and your dog seems otherwise healthy, it may indicate a minor stomach or intestinal upset or perhaps an emotional upset. You can help an occasional attack of diarrhea by regulating your dog's diet. Do not give liquids such as milk or broth in food. Provide plenty of water and thoroughly cooked starches such as rice or oatmeal. If the diarrhea does not clear up after a few days, take your dog to your veterinarian. If left untreated, diarrhea can lead to dehydration and death. If you see any blood in your dog's stool, contact your veterinarian immediately.

Preventive Medicine

You can take many preventive measures to keep your dog from becoming ill. Prevention starts with a well-balanced diet. Proper hygiene, an adequate exercise program, and a satisfactory dog-owner relationship are also important. Finally, be sure to have your puppy vaccinated against infectious diseases.

Vaccinations

Dogs are vaccinated to prevent them from contracting infectious diseases. These diseases are usually caused by bacteria or viruses and can spread rapidly throughout the dog population. Vaccinations do not always guarantee permanent protection, and annual booster shots are often necessary.

Reputable breeders vaccinate their puppies before selling them and should supply you with a record of all medical treatments. Three or four weeks must pass before an immunization becomes fully effective. You should keep a record of all of your dog's immunizations. (You will need this record if you plan to travel abroad with your dog.) These records remind you of the need for booster shots.

Canine distemper was once second only to rabies as the most dangerous dog disease known. As a highly contagious virus, it spreads through the urine, feces, saliva, and even nasal discharge of the infected animal. The virus may also be carried on blankets, brushes, and clothing. Now, however, dogs vaccinated against distemper will not contract the disease easily.

If the puppy's mother was properly vaccinated against distemper, she is able to immunize her newborn puppies passively. Such immunization lasts through nursing. After weaning, the puppies will need additional vaccinations. Bear in mind that canine distemper is dangerous and can be very difficult to treat. Thus, vaccinating your dog is extremely important.

Early symptoms of distemper include high fever, diarrhea, dry cough, depression, and watery discharge from the eyes and nose. Advanced symptoms may include cramps, loss of equilibrium, twitching of leg and facial muscles, partial paralysis, and convulsive seizures. Vaccinations and booster shots are the only effective protection against this disease. Canine distemper is almost always fatal to a young dog that has not been immunized. In older dogs, the disease may cause damage of the central nervous system.

Canine hepatitis should not be confused with human hepatitis. Canine hepatitis is caused by a virus that primarily attacks the liver and gastrointestinal tract. Dogs contract this virus in much the same manner as they do canine distemper. Although humans may carry the virus on their clothing, they cannot catch it. Vaccinated dogs rarely contract this disease. Canine hepatitis is almost always fatal to an unvaccinated puppy, however. Veterinarians can sometimes save an adult dog.

The symptoms of canine hepatitis include high fever, diarrhea, inflammation of the nasal passages, severe thirst, listlessness, and liver inflammation that makes the abdomen sensitive to the touch. A dog with canine hepatitis also tends to arch its back and rub its belly on the floor in an attempt to relieve the pain in its liver and stomach. Canine hepatitis develops very rapidly; a dog may appear healthy one day and very ill the next.

Leptospirosis is caused by bacteria transmitted through the urine of rats, mice, or an infected dog. Dogs must ingest the bacteria to contract the disease, which attacks the kidneys and liver.

The symptoms of leptospirosis are very similar to those of canine distemper and canine hepatitis. However, leptospirosis usually causes a kidney infection that changes the color and odor of the urine. The urine of an infected dog has a deep yellow-to-orange color and a strong, offensive odor.

Leptospirosis causes a dog great pain. If not treated in its early stages, it is almost always fatal. On very rare occasions, leptospirosis has been transmitted to humans. Vaccinations against this disease are the only way to protect your dog, yourself, and your family.

Parainfluenza refers to various viruses that can infect the upper respiratory system. Also known as kennel cough, it causes inflammation of the trachea and the bronchi. It commonly occurs whenever and wherever dogs congregate. If you plan to board your dog in a kennel or an animal hospital, you should see that it is vaccinated against these diseases.

Rabies is a viral infection that attacks the nervous system of all warm-blooded animals, including humans. It is usually transmitted through a bite in which the infected saliva of a rabid animal enters the victim's body. The virus also can be contracted if the saliva makes contact with an open wound.

Early symptoms of rabies include behavioral changes. An infected dog may be irritable one minute and friendly the next. Later symptoms include frequent urination and attempts to bite or eat foreign objects such as wood and stones. The dog then becomes vicious, drools excessively, and has difficulty swallowing. Finally, the dog becomes paralyzed, cannot eat or drink, and dies shortly thereafter.

Every dog should be vaccinated against rabies. Because rabies is dangerous to humans as well as dogs, the disease is considered a public health hazard. Any suspicion of rabies should be reported to public health authorities.

Parvovirus is carried and transmitted in much the same way as canine distemper. Puppies should be vaccinated before their fourteenth week.

Two forms of parvovirus are known. One causes an inflammation of the heart muscles of very young puppies. Infected animals quickly collapse and die of heart failure. The more common form, parvoviral enteritis, is characterized by constant vomiting of a foamy, yellow-brown liquid and bloody, foul-smelling diarrhea. Patting the abdomen of an infected dog will cause it to wince in pain. Parvoviral enteritis occurs in dogs of all ages and results in heavy loss of fluids. This leads to severe dehydration and death within a few days.

If the disease is detected early enough, an unvaccinated dog can be saved by intense treatment with infusions and antibiotics. However, immunization against parvovirus is the best way to protect your dog.

Note: The vaccination against parvovirus must be repeated frequently to be fully effective. Yearly boosters are recommended.

Vaccination Schedule

Prior to mating: If you intend to breed your female, bring her to your veterinarian prior to her season. She can then receive any necessary booster shots and have her stool checked for worms. This will give her puppies passive

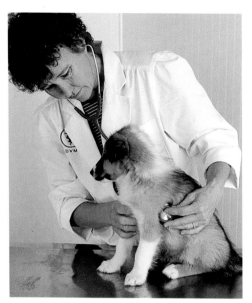

It is important to establish a good relationship with your veterinarian early in your dog's life.

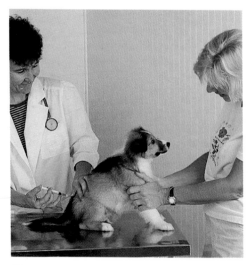

Your puppy must be vaccinated against infectious diseases.

immunity for about four to six weeks, provided she is able to nurse them.

Temporary immunizations: At four to six weeks of age, a puppy's passive immunity (conveyed by milk from the mother) begins to wear off. Your veterinarian will then administer a series of immunizations that require periodic boosters. Your puppy should receive shots against distemper, canine hepatitis, leptospirosis, parainfluenza, and parvovirus. Then every three or four weeks, until your puppy is four months old, it should receive the necessary booster shots.

Booster shots: By having your dog vaccinated regularly, you can provide it maximum protection against these infectious diseases. Your veterinarian will explain the frequency for each type of booster, which ranges from six months for parvovirus to yearly for rabies.

Internal Parasites

Roundworms are by far the most common internal parasites found in dogs. They are white, cylindrical in shape, and can grow up to 4 inches (10 cm). The adult worm embeds itself in the dog's intestinal tract to lay eggs. The eggs are then passed through the dog's stool. If ingested by another animal, the eggs will grow into adult worms inside the host and continue the cycle. Although roundworms rarely cause serious illness in adult dogs, they can be fatal to a heavily infested puppy. Roundworms are frequently found in newborn puppies if their mother was infected during pregnancy.

Symptoms of roundworm infestation include irregular appetite, diarrhea, weakness, cramps, bloated belly, and in severe cases, paralysis. In addition, the dog's anus may itch, in which case it will skid its rump across the floor in an attempt to scratch it.

Tapeworms infiltrate young and adult dogs and are very tenacious. The head of this worm has hooks and suckers that it uses to attach itself to the dog's small intestine. There it grows into a long chain of segments. The tail segment contains many eggs. Occasionally the worm releases the segments, which are passed in the dog's stool. (The segments look like grains of rice and often adhere to the hairs surrounding the anus.)

Symptoms of tapeworm infestation may take a long time to develop. Tapeworms are usually diagnosed by examining the stool. Fleas are the most common source of tapeworms, although your Sheltie may also get them from eating infected, uncooked meat (especially pork and lamb). Your veterinarian will treat tapeworms with a medication specifically for this disease.

Heartworm infestation is very serious and can be fatal if not treated promptly. Heartworms live within the heart and parts of the lungs. They cause the heart to work harder. As a result, the dog's heart ages rapidly and eventually weakens.

Heartworms are transmitted by mosquitoes that carry the worms' larvae. When the mosquito bites a dog, the larvae can enter the dog's bloodstream. The larvae take about six months to develop into mature worms.

The life cycle of the tapeworm. Egg-filled segments are passed out in the dog's feces where they are picked up by fleas, which may then be ingested by a dog. Uncooked meat or fish may also be a source of tapeworm eggs.

TIP

Flea Elimination

Solving a very bad flea problem usually takes a multipronged approach. In cases of severe infestations, I recommend the following approach:

✔ Dip your pet to eliminate the majority of adult fleas on the dog.

✔ Simultaneously, have your carpets cleaned to eliminate potential food, and launder all bedding and other washable items that may harbor fleas.

✔ Use a residual spray or IGR to prevent a recurrence of the problem.

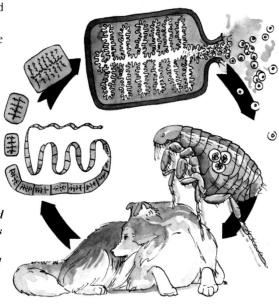

You can prevent heartworms by using Ivermectin or Milbemycin Oximine. Both of these medications are administered once a month and are effective for up to 45 days. If you should forget to give your Sheltie its medication on the designated day of the month, you would have about 15 additional days to remember to administer it, and the dog would still be protected. Unlike previously used daily heartworm medications, Ivermectin and Milbemycin Oximine will not further hurt an already infested dog. Both of these drugs are available through your veterinarian.

Treating a dog that already has heartworm is difficult and can be costly, while preventing them is easy and will cost significantly less in the long run. If you live in an area where heartworms are known to occur, have your dog tested. Consult your veterinarian about the administration of a heartworm preventative.

There are also many other forms of worms including hookworms, kidney worms, lung worms, and whipworms. Each type has different symptoms and will often require special medication. For this reason, you should contact your veterinarian promptly if you suspect your Sheltie is infested. Owners can do more damage than good to their dogs when they experiment with worming medications.

Many puppies are wormed before leaving the breeder. You should obtain a written record of worming for your veterinarian. When you bring your puppy to the veterinarian for a checkup or for its booster shots, bring a sample of its stool in a plastic bag. Your veterinarian will examine the stool for evidence of infestation.

External Parasites

Fleas are the most common of canine parasites. The images of fleas that most of us grew up with are those of cartoon dogs, rubbing their bottoms across the floor in an attempt to eliminate those singing, jumping, dancing fleas that have staked a claim to the dog like miners during a gold rush. We remember the dogs comically running in circles, scratching their backs, or chomping on their coats like a lawn mower in a vain attempt to rid themselves of those cute, tiny nuisances, which when they bit, had very large teeth. Unfortunately, flea infestations are no laughing matter.

The life cycle of the heartworm. Mosquitoes carry the larvae and pass them into the bloodstream. The larvae grow in the dog's heart.

Fleas can enter your home even if your Sheltie does not venture outside. They can hop in from outside or even hitch a ride on a human. Unfortunately, once you get fleas, they are often very difficult to eliminate. The larvae can remain dormant for an astonishingly long period of time and can withstand severe environmental conditions.

The life cycle of the flea, from egg to larvae to adult, is between three and six weeks. To get rid of fleas in your house, you must break this cycle. This usually means that you will have to repeat your initial efforts in several weeks in order to kill the new adults that were not destroyed the first time around when they were larvae.

You can check your dog for the presence of fleas by parting its coat, exposing its skin, and looking for the following characteristics. Look for bits of brown dust that, when wiped with a wet paper towel, dissolve into a red liquid (digested blood excreted by fleas). Seek out signs of irritation such as reddened skin. If you see small, fast-moving brown shapes, they are probably fleas. You should also check your Sheltie's bedding for the presence of flea dust or fleas.

Strangely enough, the primary flea infesting dogs in North America and large areas of Europe is the cat flea. Under normal conditions, this flea spends most of its adult life on the host animal, and this is where it lays its eggs. Some of the eggs will fall off of the dog. Therefore, the eggs can be found wherever your pet spends time—in the dog's bedding, in carpets, or in the yard.

You can use several methods to kill or discourage fleas. These include collars, shampoos, dips, room and yard sprays, foggers, and powders. To complicate matters even further, most of these contain a variety of natural or synthetic pesticides, or sometimes both. Some

have residual properties, which means that they are formulated to last a long time. Others are designed to break down rapidly into inert chemicals once they have done their job. Some of these products will kill fleas on contact. Others are insect growth regulators (IGRs) that prevent flea eggs from hatching and the larvae from growing into egg-laying adults.

In addition, researchers have made many recent scientific advances in the development of pesticides and their delivery systems. With each of these come some good as well as bad points. The following list describes some of the most current flea-control chemicals commercially manufactured. Sometimes a product may contain two or more of these chemicals to combine fast-acting pesticides with those that are long lasting.

Pyrethrins: These chemicals, which are extracted from flowers, have been used for many, many years. They act on the nervous system of adult fleas, killing them very rapidly. However, they have no residual properties by themselves. They have a very low toxicity to humans and animals and can therefore be used relatively safely. Some companies produce a microencapsulated (time-release) form that does offer longer-lasting results.

Permethrin: This is a synthetic pyrethrin that has become very widely used in recent years because it is claimed to be effective against both fleas and ticks (particularly those that carry Lyme disease). Permethrin is absorbed into the skin of the dog and is spread through the fat layer. Some dogs are very sensitive to this. While permethrin is known to have residual properties, it does not act fast. Therefore, many times Permethrin is used in combination with pyrethrins to get the best of both worlds.

Organophosphates: These are usually considered heavy-duty insecticides. As such, they are usually toxic to both humans and animals. As a result, the trend has been to use these as a last result.

Methoprene: This is an insect hormone that interrupts the life cycle of the flea by preventing the larvae from maturing into adults. Because it is a hormone, it is not considered a poison. However, it does prevent the fleas from reproducing. Because of this, Methoprene takes several weeks before its effects are noticed. It does not kill the egg-laying adults that are initially present. These will continue to survive until they die of natural or other causes.

Flea infestations should not be taken lightly. Be sure to treat your Sheltie with the proper flea-control product.

Imidacloprid: This chemical is available in liquids applied topically (to the skin). Imidacloprid kills on contact. This insecticide will wash off if your dog goes swimming or is bathed. It is not absorbed into the bloodstream and has a long-lasting effect (about one month). It is selectively toxic to insects, so it is not toxic to humans or animals.

Fipronil: This insecticide works similarly to Imidacloprid, but it is not water soluble and will not come off if your dog gets wet. It can be removed with alcohol or with shampoo. Fipronil will attach itself to the oil in the dog's skin and coat. Therefore, not bathing the dog for two days prior to treatment is important. This allows sufficient oil to be left on the dog's skin and coat to absorb the chemical. Fipronil can be safely used on pups, kittens, dogs, and cats.

Pyripoxyfen: This material is similar to Fipronil but is approved for use only on dogs. This chemical is found in combination with Permethrin to give residual effects against fleas and ticks and in combination with IGRs.

Lufenuron: This is an IGR that prevents fleas in their various stages from producing chitin. Chitin makes up approximately 30 percent of the flea's body weight and is the major component of the flea's exoskeleton. When Lufenuron is used, flea eggs are unable to hatch. The teeth of the pupae inside the egg are made of chitin, and they are therefore unable to eat their way out of the egg. Likewise when the larvae molt, they are not able to produce new exoskeletons and rapidly perish. This material does not have any adulticidal activity. It is available only through a veterinary prescription. Unlike all of the other chemicals listed in this section, Lufenuron is administered orally in the pet's food. It comes in tablet form for dogs and in a liquid suspension for cats. It is effective for one month. The dosage is absorbed into the intestinal tract of the dog and transferred, via the bloodstream, to the outer tissue layers. If an adult flea then bites the treated dog, it ingests the IGR and its progeny will not be able to develop into adults. Because this

During your grooming sessions, spread out your Sheltie's coat to expose the skin. In this way, you can look for signs of fleas or any potential skin disorders.

chemical affects only the eggs and larvae, breaking the life cycle and reducing a significant portion of the flea infestation will take four to five weeks.

As you can see, flea control products come in a wide variety of forms, and while some are available in retail outlets, others are available only through a prescription from your veterinarian.

Not all flea control methods are 100 percent effective. You will probably have to combine several approaches to get satisfactory results. You must also keep in mind that regional differences exist among fleas. You may want to seek the advice of a local veterinarian or dog groomer to learn about what is effective in your area. You may also have to switch your approach from year to year because using the same products over and over can lead to a buildup of immunity among the fleas.

Regardless of the method you choose for treating fleas, the first line of defense is through regular vacuuming and emptying of the vacuum bags. This will help to eliminate eggs and to reduce the food sources for the flea larvae. If you catch the flea problem early

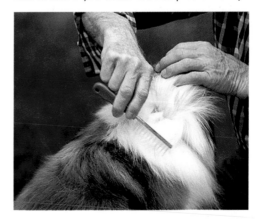

enough, you may be able to deal with fleas by using powders and sprays that you can apply directly to your dog and areas of your house where your dog frequently stays.

Lice, like all other external parasites, burrow into one area, suck blood, and cause irritation. You can see clusters of eggs on your dog's hairs if it is infested. Lice can be very dangerous, so bring your dog to your veterinarian promptly if you spot them. The doctor can eliminate the lice by using an insecticide dip.

Ticks are bloodsuckers that, once embedded, hang on tenaciously. Ticks can carry serious diseases such as Rocky Mountain spotted fever. Another infection transmitted through ticks is Lyme disease. In recent years, the number of infected dogs has risen dramatically in the northeastern and midwestern portions of the United States. A dog infected with Lyme disease (named after the Connecticut town where the ailment was first noted in humans) exhibits symptoms of stiffness, pain, fever, inflammation of joints, and rashes. If caught early enough, Lyme disease can be cured with antibiotic therapy. Tetracycline is the drug of choice.

Another tick-borne disease that has long affected animals and is now appearing in both dogs and humans is babesiosis. In dogs, babesiosis causes fever, anorexia, lethargy, depression, pallor, and rapid pulse rate.

The increase in reported cases of tick-borne diseases is most likely due to the increasing population of host animals (raccoons, deer, and opossums) moving into areas in which they have been scarce before. The ticks will then leave the animal it has infected and will seek a new host such as a dog or a human.

Humans cannot catch a tick-borne disease from a dog. However, they can become infected by the same tick that is transmitting the disease. Eradicating ticks from all areas is impossible. However, try to keep your dog away from known tick-infested areas such as open fields and woods. Inspecting your dog for ticks each time it returns to the house is also a good practice. Be sure to check inside the ears and between the toes, for these are a tick's favorite location.

To remove a tick, first wash the infected area with alcohol, which helps to loosen the tick's grasp. When you have loosened it somewhat, place a pair of tweezers squarely over the tick and carefully lift it off. Be careful not to pull the body apart; you must remove it whole. If the head remains under the dog's skin, it can cause an infection. Once you have removed the tick, place it into the middle of your toilet and flush. However, if you suspect the tick of carrying a disease, you should place it into a tightly sealed jar and bring it to your veterinarian for examination.

Never attempt to remove a tick with a lighted match or with your bare fingers. You can contract tick-borne diseases from contact with the tick. If your dog begins to show signs of tick-borne diseases, take your dog to a veterinarian immediately.

Mites are parasites no larger than a pinhead. Like fleas, they cause intense itching. Hence, a dog that scratches and chews at its skin may not be suffering from flea infestation. Symptoms such as red dots, pimples, damp spots, crusty scaly skin, greasy skin, or loss of hair can mean eczema, mites, nutritional deficiencies, hormonal imbalances, allergies, and so on. Consult your veterinarian regarding the diagnosis and treatment of these ailments.

Mange, a serious skin disease, can exhibit the same symptoms because it is caused by mites. The two principal forms of mange are sarcoptic mange and demodectic mange. Sarcoptic mange is usually easier to recognize because it makes the dog more miserable and causes more scratching. The affected area becomes red and full of bloody sores and scabs. The skin thickens and feels leathery. The dog's hair sheds completely in the affected area. The disease then begins to spread. The dog produces an odor similar to that of strong cheese or that associated with a foot problem.

Demodectic mange is harder to detect because sometimes it results in only slight hair loss and some reddening and inflammation of the affected skin. Sometimes bloody pimples form that can burst and become infected. This condition does not always cause a great deal of itching or irritation. The only signs of demodectic mange may be a small lesion about ½ inch (1 cm) in diameter marked by hair loss or a small bald spot.

Your veterinarian can identify either type of mange by taking skin scrapings and examining them under a microscope.

Other Skin Disorders

Additional skin disorders include allergies, eczema, and ringworm. Allergic symptoms may be similar to those of other skin ailments: inflammation, itching, pimples, flaking or scaling, and sometimes hair loss. Treatment usually takes time; first your veterinarian must diagnose the specific cause.

Eczema is a general name for several different skin irritations. Eczema occurs in either wet or dry patches. It may have many causes, including dietary deficiencies of vitamin A and fat, exposure to dampness or excessive heat, hormone imbalance, and parasites.

Ringworm is not a worm but a fungus. It affects the outer layer of a dog's skin. It may cause inflammation, itching, hair loss, and scabby areas. It may be transmitted from an infected dog to a human, so prompt veterinary treatment is essential.

Note: If ringworm is suspected in a human, it should also be diagnosed and treated at once.

Digestive Disorders

Constipation

Constipation occurs when solid waste products that cannot be easily passed build up in the dog's digestive tract. Generally, this can be relieved by changing the dog's diet and by including a mild laxative. Half a cup of lukewarm milk hourly can also be most effective. You should reduce dry bulk foods in your dog's diet until the stool is normal.

Constipation may also be caused by eating an indigestible object, such as a small toy or a stone. If you suspect this, call your veterinarian immediately. Do not give your dog a laxative if you suspect a foreign object. This may require surgery.

Enteritis

Inflammation of the intestine may be caused by bacteria, poisons, worms, ulcers, the swallowing of sharp objects, and so on. Regardless of the cause, any inflammation of the intestinal tract is called enteritis. This condition may be accompanied by diarrhea or foul-smelling stools. Enteritis may cause the dog much discomfort, resulting in its lying in unusual and contorted positions when at rest. Almost all intestinal ailments require professional care.

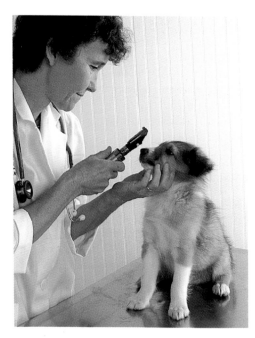

Therefore, if these symptoms appear, contact your veterinarian immediately.

Throat/Respiratory Ailments

Dogs can contract most common throat and respiratory ailments, including coughs, asthma, bronchitis, laryngitis, and pneumonia. Dogs do not suffer from the common cold but are subject to a similar respiratory ailment. Symptoms include runny nose, thin mucous discharge from the eyes, slight fever, chills, coughing, and sneezing.

Tonsillitis

Tonsillitis, an inflammation of the tonsils, is usually caused by an infection. A dog with tonsillitis may run a high fever, refuse to eat, drool, and vomit frequently and violently. Your

Collie-eye is an inherited disorder.

veterinarian can treat tonsillitis with appropriate medication; only rarely is surgery required.

Parainfluenza

Frequently called kennel cough, parainfluenza is a common respiratory ailment in dogs. It responds to treatment readily, especially in the early stages. Immunization, with annual boosters, has also proven effective (see page 43).

Pneumonia

Once a common killer of dogs, pneumonia is now treated successfully with antibiotics. Pneumonia is characterized by a cough, shallow breathing, nasal discharge, loss of appetite, and high fever.

Most respiratory ailments can be treated with antibiotics. Take your dog to your veterinarian if it shows signs of severe respiratory problems.

Eye Disorders

While few Shetland Sheepdogs suffer from major eye disorders, collie-eye seems to be the most common. The collie-eye abnormality is an inherited ocular defect present from birth. The disease does have associated symptoms that can be detected only by a veterinarian. The eyes of the affected Sheltie may be small or more deeply set.

While visual loss occurs in fewer than 1 percent of the affected dogs, if the disease causes a detachment of the retina, it will cause blindness. Checking for inherited eye disorders before breeding your Sheltie is wise.

Ear Ailments

Shelties suffer from few ear ailments. However, if you suspect an ear problem, leave the dog's ear alone and contact your veterinarian. An inexperienced owner who probes too far into the sensitive ear canal can cause the dog additional damage.

Symptoms of ear disorders include persistent shaking of the head, rubbing the ears with paws or on the floor, cocking the head at an unusual angle, and any type of discharge from the ear. The insides of the dog's ears may appear reddish and inflamed.

Collie Nose

While this disease is not believed to be inherited, it is present from birth. Collie nose is an abnormal reaction of the skin to sunlight and occurs most commonly in Collies, Shetland Sheepdogs, and German Shepherds. This disease, which is characterized by dermatitis or eczema, primarily affects the dog's nose, eyes, and adjacent areas.

The progress of the disease is slow. At first, it may appear to be a light reddening of the muzzle skin. As the disease progresses, the skin on the bridge of the nose becomes markedly irritated, and lesions may begin to occur. The dog may contract conjunctivitis. The skin around the face and eyes becomes pink to bright red and sore. This disease can be controlled but not cured by the application of topical medications. Lesions caused by this disease are more intense in the summer and subside during the winter. This condition can also be

The veterinarian should check your Sheltie's inner ear.

greatly improved by keeping your dog away from sunlight.

Other Disorders

Hip Dysplasia

Hip dysplasia is a developmental disease of the hip joints. This ailment occurs most commonly in young dogs of larger breeds. Therefore, Shelties are not as susceptible as their larger cousins, the Collie. The disease itself is due to a hip socket malformation that does not allow for the proper fit of the head of the femur.

At birth, the hips of a dog with severe hip dysplasia appear normal. Signs of the disorder do not appear until the dog is five months or older. The optimum age for a definite diagnosis is between 24 and 36 months. Hip dysplasia results in painful inflammation of the hip joint, which leads to permanent physical damage, including lameness and loss of the use of the back legs.

Veterinarians can surgically correct the shape of the hip socket. Another surgical procedure, known as total hip replacement, has been highly successful. Unfortunately, these procedures are performed by only a limited number of specialists, and they can be quite costly. It is estimated that only a small percentage of Shetland Sheepdogs suffer from this disease, which has low to moderate heritability.

Shock

Shock is a serious condition that results from a traumatic physical or emotional experience. The most common cause is an automobile accident. A dog in shock may appear asleep, or it may be semiconscious. Symptoms vary according to the severity of the condition. Breathing may be shallow, the dog's body may be cold, and its pulse may be rapid.

If your dog is in shock, try to calm it in a soft voice, pet it reassuringly, and if possible, cover it with a blanket or an article of clothing. Because the actions of a dog in shock are unpredictable, use caution in handling it. Take it to a veterinarian immediately.

Poisoning

It is important for you to call directory assistance now and obtain the telephone number of the nearest poison control center. Keep this number easily accessible in case of emergency.

One of the most common poisons ingested by dogs is rodent poison (these are usually blood anticoagulants). Symptoms include blood in the vomit, stool, and urine and nosebleeds. Such poisoning can quickly prove fatal. A veterinarian can help only if the dog has ingested a small amount of the poison.

Some pesticides are extremely poisonous. Store all pesticides safely, and keep dogs away from treated plants for at least two weeks after spraying. Poisoning results in diarrhea, cramps, shortness of breath, and dizziness.

Another common cause of poisoning is ingesting antifreeze. Dogs seem to love its taste. Although antifreeze itself is not poisonous, the dog's body converts it into several toxic substances that can lead to irreversible kidney damage and eventual death. If you see your dog drink antifreeze, immediately take the dog to your veterinarian.

Nursing a Sick Dog

Learn the proper way to hold your dog, for you may need to perform various medical procedures by yourself. Lay the dog's head in the crook of your arm. Hold it firmly, leaving your other arm free. While you do this, be sure to talk quietly to your Sheltie to help calm and reassure it.

Use only a minimal amount of pressure to pry open the dog's jaws when administering a pill.

Place the pill in the back of the dog's mouth, but do not force it into the throat, which could cause the dog to choke.

You should also know how to take your dog's temperature. You will need a regular rectal thermometer and some KY or petroleum jelly. Because you take the dog's temperature rectally, you may need someone to help you.

The normal body temperature of an adult Shetland Sheepdog is between 100.5 and 102.5°F (38–39.2°C). The temperature is slightly higher in younger dogs and slightly lower in older ones. If your dog is placid, lubricate a digital thermometer (glass thermometers can break) with KY or petroleum jelly, lift the dog's tail, and slip in the thermometer. You can remove it after two or three minutes. Wash the thermometer in *cold* water when you are done.

You should also learn to take your dog's pulse. Feeling the pulse on the inside of the front paw or on the thigh on the heart side is best. An adult Sheltie has a pulse rate of 75 to 95 beats per minute. In younger dogs, the pulse is slightly quicker. In a calm, healthy Sheltie, the pulse is strong and steady.

Learn how to give your dog medication. Powdered medications can be mixed with water and drawn into a syringe without a needle on it. Open the lips on the side of your dog's mouth near its molars. While loosely holding the dog's muzzle shut, let the liquid flow slowly into the space between the molars. Allow your dog time to swallow until all of the liquid is taken. If the dog refuses to take a pill, put it inside some hamburger or other meat.

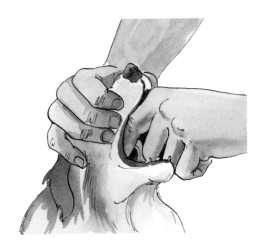

If this fails, you may have to force your dog to swallow a pill. Hold the dog's upper jaw and, while exerting mild pressure, raise its head. This should cause the dog's mouth to open. Quickly place the pill onto the back of its tongue, hold its mouth closed, tilt its head upward, and rub the dog's throat in a downward direction.

Saying Goodbye

Euthanasia is the act by which a veterinarian can painlessly induce death, ending the suffering of a terminally ill animal. When you must make the painful decision of having your dog put to sleep, consider the animal's feelings as well as your own. This is never an easy choice. It will probably be made only after deep soul-searching. A caring veterinarian will understand the choices you may have to make and will be supportive and open for discussion. However, the decision must be yours.

BREEDING SHELTIES

Breeding Objectives

The objectives of dog breeding should always be to produce and raise puppies that will uphold the quality of the physical characteristics and the temperament of the breed. However, some unscrupulous breeders seek only to make a quick dollar on inferior litters. It is also too true that reckless breeding will increase in proportion to the popularity of the breed. Unfortunately, the Shetland Sheepdog is not an exception to the rule.

With the increased popularity of the Shetland Sheepdog, we are beginning to see the result of these unprincipled breeding practices. We are beginning to see changes in the Shelties' physical size. Mainly, a greater number of Shelties are larger than 16 inches (40 cm) (the standard's maximum height) at the shoulder. In addition, we are beginning to see an increase in Shelties with behavioral abnormalities. In the end, not only will these breeders ruin the reputation of the breed, but they will also increase the already heartbreaking number of unwanted dogs.

Serious breeders wish to improve their dogs through selective breeding with quality dogs from other well-run kennels. Their main goal is to develop a bloodline of their own, one strong in the qualities that best exemplify the Shetland Sheepdog standard.

Serious breeders strive to meet the AKC standard.

The Shetland Sheepdog standard is a complete written description of the perfect Sheltie: how it should look, act, and move. Of course, no one has ever produced the perfect Sheltie. Most likely, no one ever will. However, the standard is the goal for which serious breeders strive. The Shetland Sheepdog standard used in the United States was prepared by the American Shetland Sheepdog Association and approved by the AKC. Every breed recognized by the AKC has its own standard by which it is judged at dog shows.

If individual breeders were to produce what they considered perfect Shelties, the breed would vary widely. Without standards, each breed would quickly lose its identity. Adherence to the standard separates conscientious breeders from unscrupulous ones who are more concerned with profits than with the quality and well-being of their puppies.

Sheltie Characteristics

The following descriptions are based on my interpretation of the AKC-approved standard for Shetland Sheepdogs. However, this is not necessarily the interpretation of dog show judges. If you plan to enter your Sheltie in a conformation competition, obtain a copy of the Shetland Sheepdog standard from the AKC. Remember that if you enter your Sheltie in a show competition, only the judges' interpretation of the standard will decide the winners.

General Description: The Shetland Sheepdog is a small, alert, rough-coated, long-haired working dog. It must be sound, agile, and sturdy. The outline should be so symmetrical that no part appears out of proportion to the whole. Males should look masculine, while females should look feminine.

Size: The Shetland Sheepdog should measure between 13 and 16 inches (32.5–40 cm) at the shoulder. Shoulder height measurements are taken with the dog standing naturally with its forelegs perpendicular to the ground. The measurement is taken from the ground directly up the foreleg to the top of the shoulder blades.

Coat: Because the Sheltie was originally bred as a herding dog for the harsh climate of the Shetland Islands, its coat must be suited to keep out the weather. Shelties have a double coat. The outer coat consists of long, straight, coarse hair. The undercoat is short and furry. The combination of these two coats gives the Sheltie its full standoff quality. The hair on the Sheltie's face, feet, and tips of the ears should be smooth. The mane of the Sheltie should be thick and full.

Because males should look more masculine, their mane and frills should be more abundant than those of a female. The hair on the forelegs and hind legs are feathered, with the hind legs heavier than the forelegs on top but smooth below the hock joint (the joint equivalent to a backward knee). The hair on a Sheltie's tail should also be thick and abundant. Any excess hair on the ears, feet, or hocks may be trimmed for the show ring.

Color: There are wide variations of color in Shelties. Black, blue merle, and sable (ranging from golden to mahogany) marked with white and/or tan are all recognized color variations. (Blue merle consists of mottling of bluish gray color on the face and back.) Unacceptable color variations include rustiness in a black or blue coat, faded colors, conspicuous white spots, or over 50 percent white.

Temperament: The Shetland Sheepdog should exhibit the temperament of a herding dog. The dog should be intensely loyal, affectionate, and responsive to its owner or handler. The standard allows for a Sheltie to be "reserved toward strangers." However, the dog should show no signs of fear or cringing.

Head: The head, when viewed from the top, should "be a long, blunt wedge tapering slightly from ears to nose." The nose must always be black. The top of the skull is flat, without a prominent nuchal crest (the knotlike bone structure at the top of the skull). The cheeks of the Sheltie are flat and should smoothly curve into a "well-rounded muzzle."

The skeletal structure of the Shetland Sheepdog.

The muzzle should be the same length as the skull with the balance point at the inner corner of the eye when viewed from the side. The flattened line along the top of the Sheltie's skull should be parallel to the flat top of the muzzle but on a higher plane due to the "presence of a slight but definite stop." The underjaw should be deep and well developed. It is rounded at the chin and extends to the base of the nostril. A Sheltie's jaws are clean and powerful. When its lips are tight, the upper and lower lip meet and create a smooth seal all the way around. The teeth should be level and evenly spaced, with the dog having a scissor bite.

Eyes: A Sheltie's eyes are medium size and have dark, almond-shaped rims. The eyes must be dark. (Blue merle eyes are permissible only in blue merles.) The eyes are set at a slight angle into the skull.

Ears: This breed has small and supple ears with the tips breaking forward. The ears are located high on the skull and carried about three-quarters erect. When resting, the Sheltie will fold its ears lengthwise and throw them back into the frill.

Expression: The basic shape and contour of the head, along with the location and positioning of its eyes and ears, all combine to produce the Sheltie's expression. Under normal conditions, the expression should be "alert, gentle, intelligent, and questioning." In the presence of a stranger, the expression should be one of watchfulness and caution; however, no sign of fear should appear.

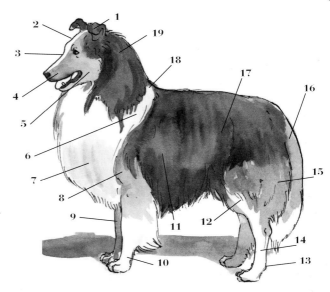

Conformation of the Shetland Sheepdog:
1. ears 2. skull 3. stop 4. muzzle 5. cheek
6. shoulder 7. chest 8. brisket 9. forequarters
10. front pastern 11. ribcage 12. stifle
13. rear pastern 14. hock 15. hindquarters
16. tail 17. loin 18. withers 19. neckline

Neck: Shelties have a muscular neck that should be arched and long enough to carry its head proudly.

Body: The body should appear moderately long as measured from the shoulder joint to the ischium (the rearmost extremity of the pelvic bone). The long appearance of the body is actually due to the proper breadth and angles of the shoulder and hindquarters. While the back of the Sheltie should be comparatively short, it must be level and well-muscled. A Shetland Sheepdog has a deep chest with the brisket reaching to the back point of the elbow. Its ribs should be well-sprung but flattened at the lower half; this allows for the free movement of the foreleg and shoulder. The abdomen of the Sheltie should be tucked up fairly well even though its coat may give the abdomen an appearance of being flat or rounded.

Forequarters: When starting at the withers (the highest point of the shoulder), the shoulder blade should slope downward and forward at a 45-degree angle to the shoulder joints. At the very top of the shoulders, the withers are separated by only the vertebrae. However, they should slope outward at an angle sufficient to allow for the spring of the ribs. The upper arm should join the shoulder blade at a 90-degree angle. The elbow joint should be located midway between the withers and the ground. When viewed from any angle, the forelegs of the Sheltie must appear straight, muscular, clean, and strong boned. The pasterns (back of the foreleg) should appear strong, flexible, and sinewy.

Feet (front and hind): The feet are oval with well-arched toes that fit tightly together. A Sheltie has deep, tough pads and hard, strong nails on its feet.

Hindquarters: There should be a slight arch at the loins. The croup (highest point of the rump) should gradually slope to the rear. The hipbone should be set at a 30-degree angle to the spine. The Sheltie should possess a broad and muscular thigh. The thighbone should be set into the pelvis at a right angle (this corresponds to the angle made by the shoulder blade and the upper arms of the forelegs). The stifle bones (which join the hind leg and the body) should be "distinctly angled at the stifle joint." The overall length of the stifle bones should be equal to or slightly longer than the thighbone. The hock joint (the next joint below the stifle) should be angular and sinewy with good, strong bones and ligaments. The hock should be short and, like the foreleg, should be straight when viewed from all angles. Dewclaws should be removed.

Tail: The tail should be long enough that when it is laid along the back edge of the hind legs, the last vertebra will touch the hock joint. When the tail is at rest, it should be carried straight down or at a slight upward curve. When alert, the Sheltie will normally lift its tail. However, the tail should not curve forward and over its back.

The hair on the Sheltie's face and on the tips of its ears should be smooth. The Sheltie's mane should be thick and full.

The only reason to breed a dog is to improve the overall breed.

Gait: When trotting, the Shetland Sheepdog should give one the impression of "effortless speed and smoothness." The proper trot will show no signs of jerkiness, stiffness, or up-and-down motion. The rear legs should appear to be the driving force. The line on which it runs must be straight and true. If all the angulation, musculature, and ligaments are correct, the rear legs of the trotting Sheltie will reach well under its body and then retract smoothly, propelling the dog forward. Proper reach of stride of the forelegs of the Sheltie likewise depends upon the proper angulation, musculature, and ligaments of the forequarters. In addition, the proper reach of stride will be achieved only if the dog has the correct width of chest and construction of the rib cage. When trotting, the front feet should be lifted only enough to clear the ground when the legs swing forward. When viewing the dog from the front, both the forelegs and hind legs should be perpendicular to the ground when the dog is walking. When trotting, the legs should become angled inward. When running swiftly, the "feet are brought so far inward toward center line of body that the tracks left show two parallel lines of footprints actually touching a center line at their inner edges." When moving, the Sheltie should not cross its feet or throw its weight from side to side.

Breeding Females

The responsibilities of a dog breeder are numerous. Before the dog is bred, the breeder must visit prospective stud dogs and spend time researching pedigrees and studying genetics. The breeder must keep the female dog in top breeding condition, help sustain her through the entire pregnancy, and then help her during delivery and raising the puppies.

If you are truly interested in breeding quality Shelties and are not discouraged by the amount of responsibility, then contact an experienced breeder. A professional can help you either breed your dog or teach you the principles of dog breeding. Under no circumstances should an amateur breed a female Sheltie.

Once you have an understanding of the principles of breeding, seek the advice of your local Shetland Sheepdog Club. This group is a valuable source of information and can help you find a suitable stud dog. The following is a very basic summary of the information you need before breeding your Sheltie.

Choosing a mate: After obtaining a list of available stud dogs from your Shetland Sheepdog Club, you should make appointments to visit as many of the breeders as possible. While visiting, keep in mind that you will be selecting the dog that best complements your female. You should study each dog for its conformation to the breed standard. Then you should ask to see the dog's pedigree. The pedigree will show you if any champions are in the stud dog's bloodline. Although breeding your female to a champion stud dog is a good start, you should place much greater emphasis on the overall quality of the dog's bloodlines.

Once you choose a stud dog, you will have to agree with the owner on a stud fee. Many times the stud dog's owner takes the pick of the litter instead of money, but this must be agreed upon ahead of time.

When is the female ready? The age at which you can first breed your female is between 16 and 18 months. However, waiting until her second or third season is usually best. She should be mature enough to cope with the physical and mental demands.

Before your female's estrus, bring her to the veterinarian to be checked for worms and for a booster shot if she has not recently had one. Make sure she is neither over- nor underweight.

When her season is near, check her daily for the swelling of her vulva and the appearance of color. The best time to breed a female is from 9 to 14 days after the first signs of color. When the swelling and color first appear, make an appointment with the owner of the stud dog to bring the female for mating. Once mating has taken place, do not separate the dogs if they are still coupled. The dogs will separate on their own without human intervention. Once they are separated, remove the female and put her into her cage or your car.

The birth of puppies: It is important to thoroughly prepare both yourself and your Sheltie for this event so that there will be as little confusion as possible when it is her time to give birth. The less confusion, the less stressful it will be on her.

Your female should be on a special whelping diet—in accordance with your veterinarian's instructions. As the next several weeks pass, she will most likely require an increasing amount of food. After about seven weeks, start to cut down on her exercise.

Introduce your female to her whelping box. Put the box into a warm, quiet spot. Line it with a thick layer of newspapers covered by a clean blanket and some cloths that can be easily changed.

The gestation period of a Shetland Sheepdog is usually nine weeks. Your female will let you know when whelping time is near. She will become restless and wander in and out of her box. She will begin to lose the hair around her breasts. This is perfectly normal. At this time, remove all distractions from around your Sheltie. Be sure you do not disturb her. Give her plenty of room. Stay nearby, speaking softly to calm her. Eventually, she will settle in her box and begin her labor, which includes heavy panting followed by visible contractions. Soon the first puppy will appear at the vulva and will slide out with the contraction.

The mother Sheltie will actually take care of the entire birth process. In most cases, you will be needed only if complications arise. When the puppy is completely out, the mother should immediately tear open the amniotic sac and shred the umbilical cord, using her teeth. She will then begin to clean the puppy by licking it. While she is licking the puppy, she may also rub her muzzle along the underside and sides of the newborn pup. This serves to massage and stimulate the puppy to begin breathing. If the mother attempts to eat the afterbirth, allow it, for this is perfectly natural. The afterbirth is high in nutrients. Eating it will promote

the production of milk as well as encourage further labor for the birth of the next puppy.

The puppies should be born at about half-hour intervals. The average Sheltie litter is about seven puppies, so it will take about seven to eight hours from the start of labor until the last puppy is born. If you have an unusually large litter, you may have to help the mother feed her young by bottle-feeding the additional puppies. Commercial milk supplements are available at most pet stores.

On rare occasions, complications may arise. Your veterinarian, who has taken care of your Sheltie through her pregnancy, should be on hand in case an emergency arises during labor.

You are now responsible for taking care of the puppies. At four weeks, they can be weaned off the mother's milk and you must provide them with food. At six or seven weeks, have them checked and vaccinated by your veterinarian. At seven weeks, you must also find them quality homes. Contact the Shetland Sheepdog Club about potential buyers.

Prior to mating, introduce your female to the male. Be sure to keep both dogs on a leash in case you have to separate them quickly.

UNDERSTANDING SHELTIES

Early History

Although the Shetland Sheepdog clearly has older roots, the first clear records of its existence date back to the early 1800s. At about this time, visitors to the Shetland Islands brought back to the mainland of England and Scotland small farm dogs called toonies. These toonies that were being used to care for sheep in the Shetlands were described as a small breed of Collie. By using this description, little doubt exists that the toonies were what we now call Shetland Sheepdogs.

Today's Sheltie directly descends from the small sheepherding dog used in the northern islands of Scotland. The harsh climate and rough terrain of the islands do not make them the ideal location to raise an abundance of large cattle. Vegetation is sparse on these islands, and there are few places to hide from the severe North Sea storms that frequent the island. With limited food sources and space requirements, it would be almost impossible for large species of cattle, or any other large land animal, to survive a long time in the Shetlands.

Luckily, nature has a way of solving its own problems. In order for animals to survive in the Shetland Islands, they had to be adaptable.

Shelties are naturally curious dogs.

Smaller, hardier animals could survive in this harsh environment. They require less food and can find shelter in many more places than can larger animals. So, after generation upon generation of evolution, literally all of the animals common to the Shetland Islands have become smaller and hardier than their cousins on the mainland. This reduction in size can be seen in both the domestic and wild animals that inhabit the islands. Besides the Shetland Sheepdog, one of the best known examples of this is the Shetland pony. Like the diminutiveness of the Sheltie, the small size of the Shetland pony is very much a result of the islands' environment.

The rugged landscape and severe weather of the islands rule out commercial farming, while the isolated location of the Shetlands make them an impractical place to establish many factories. For a long time, the raising of livestock has logically been the major industry of the Shetland Islands.

The types of livestock that can be effectively raised on the Shetland Islands must be able to adapt to the terrain and climate. After generations of being raised on the islands, the domestic cattle and sheep evolved into miniature versions of their mainland predecessors.

While the exact origins of the Shetland Sheepdog are unknown, it is generally believed that this breed descended from a small working dog that was also the progenitor of the modern show Collie. Accentuating the effects of the island environment is the fact that the small working dog was also crossed with other small breeds believed to have been residing in, or indigenous to, the islands.

How long the evolution of the modern-day Shetland Sheepdog took to complete is not known for no written records exist. Because these dogs were bred in the relative isolation of the islands, it took a long time before the breed became known to the dog enthusiasts of the outside world. Thus, not until 1909 did the Sheltie obtain its initial recognition by the English Kennel Club when it was classified as a Shetland Collie. In 1914, the breed obtained a separate classification and has since been known as the Shetland Sheepdog. In 1915, the first Challenge Certificate was awarded to the breed.

Over the years, several Shetland Sheepdog clubs have been formed. Unfortunately, their history has always been one of controversy over variations in the acceptable size and type of the breed. The oldest club, the Shetland Sheepdog Club of the Islands, was founded in 1908. Their standard asked for a "rough collie in miniature" with a height not to exceed 15 inches (38 cm). The Scottish Shetland Sheepdog Club, founded in 1909, at first requested an "ordinary collie in miniature," with an ideal height of 12 inches (30 cm). Later this club changed its standard to "a modern show collie in miniature" and changed the dog's ideal height to 13½ inches (34 cm). The English Shetland Sheepdog Club, an offshoot of the Scottish club, was founded in 1914. Like its parent club, its members also had their own opinion as to the ideal Sheltie. The English

Club called for "approximately a show collie in miniature" with an ideal height of 12 inches (30 cm). This was later changed to an acceptable range of 12 to 15 inches (30–38 cm), the ideal being 13½ inches (34 cm). Adding to the controversy was the British Breeders Association, an offspring of the English club. They called for "a show collie in miniature" while maintaining the same heights as their parent club.

Finally in 1930, both the Scottish and English clubs revised their standards to read "should resemble a collie (rough) in miniature." Even today, some variations still exist among the different clubs in the British Isles; however, these differences are now in a much more refined form.

The different standards among the various clubs reflected the breeders' struggle to obtain and perpetuate the ideal size and type. As mentioned, the progenitor working Collie was bred to other smaller breeds to reduce its size. The crossbreeding risked introducing characteristics contradictory to the true Collie type. Crossbreeding the working Collie with small Spaniels, for instance, resulted in undesirable traits such as wavy coats, houndlike ears, long bodies, large round eyes, and wagging tails. On the other hand, these Spaniels also brought the beneficial characteristics of calm and devoted dispositions. It is also believed that a little yellow dog from Iceland that had a dark muzzle and pricked ears also influenced the breed.

To counteract the undesirable traits that were beginning to appear, crosses with modern Collies were made. This cross was responsible for improving the head properties, such as ear type and expression, as well as enabling the breeder to obtain the beautiful, weatherresistant coat. However, even this crossbreeding had its faults, such as legginess, excessive size, loss of substance, and imbalance.

Thus, breeders had to breed these new smaller Collies in such a way as to produce a dog having all the traits associated with a correct Collie. At the same time, they attempted to keep the correct balance and size that we associate with our modern-day Sheltie.

The Shetland Sheepdog Standard presently approved by the Kennel Club of Great Britain has essentially the same requirements set forth by the AKC. If you plan to register your Sheltie in England or show your dog internationally, obtaining a copy of the British Standard would be wise.

The major difference between the standards of Kennel Club of Great Britain and AKC lies once again in the Sheltie's height. The British standard states that the ideal height for Shelties is 14½ inches (37 cm) for males and 14 inches (35.5 cm) for females. The American Kennel Club standard calls for a height of between 13 and 16 inches (32.5–40 cm) at the shoulder. Any height measurement over one inch (2.5 em) above the ideal is to be considered a serious fault.

Shelties in America

While records exist of the Sheltie being brought to New York in 1911, not until 1929 was the American Shetland Sheepdog Association (ASSA) formed. When developing the Shetland Sheepdog standard for AKC approval, the ASSA combined the best of all of the British standards. As stated, the current AKC-approved standard specifies a height from 13 to 16 inches (32.5–40 cm).

The first Sheltie breeders in the United States encountered problems like those in the British Isles. In their attempts to improve the physical characteristics of the breed, the American Shelties were crossed with their larger cousins, the show Collie. In order to maintain the small size associated with the Sheltie, crosses with only smaller Collies were made. However, like in Great Britain, this practice resulted in oversized dogs.

Since then, improvement of the Shetland Sheepdog has been done only through selective breeding. Now the common practice is to breed Shelties that have some weaker traits with dogs of the same breed that are stronger in the targeted physical or behavioral characteristics. As a result, the modern show Shetland Sheepdog has become a beautifully balanced dog that has the type, weather-resistant coat, and expression of a Collie combined with the Sheltie's smaller size, character, and charm.

The Nature of Shelties

Now that we have examined the origins of the Sheltie, you see how it acquired its size, shape, and color. To understand the Sheltie's behavior patterns, however, we must examine the process by which dogs evolved and were domesticated. All dogs, regardless of breed, trace their ancestry to a form of wild dog or wolf.

Wild dogs have a specially structured society. Most of their behavior rituals allow each member of the pack to live in harmony with the others. With the passing of countless generations of dogs, some of these rituals became instinctive. Modern domesticated dogs exhibit many of these instinctive behavior patterns,

including marking of territory and establishing a ranking order among human companions.

It is believed that dogs were the first domesticated animal; evidence indicates that this process began about 12,000 years ago. Humans probably tamed wolves or wild dogs to assist them in hunting. Hunting practices and social structures of both humans and dogs were probably very similar at this time.

As dogs became domestic, they lost some of their instinctive behavior patterns while others

The lush, thick coat of the Sheltie hides a well-muscled, compact body that a sheepdog needs when herding livestock.

were retained. Which traits were lost and which were retained depends on the specific breed and how it was domesticated. As you know, Shetland Sheepdogs were originally bred as herding dogs, as were most of their domestic ancestors. Thus, Shelties naturally display

There are few breeds that can match the elegance, expression, and beauty of the
Shetland Sheepdog.

excellent herding and watchdog skills. While not all of our modern Shelties exhibit all the skills necessary to be an effective herding dog, many of these traits have become part of this breed's instinctive behavioral pattern. An example of this can be seen in the natural movements and temperament of the Sheltie. The physical structure of the Sheltie enables the dog to exhibit strength, speed, grace, and jumping power—all necessary attributes for the successful herding dog. Shelties are also instinctively loyal and affectionate to their owners while showing reserve, but not nervousness, to strangers. All of these traits, with the addition of the Sheltie's alertness, are common to all Shetland Sheepdogs. Yet these features are not seen in all breeds of dogs.

Because Shelties and their domestic ancestors were herding dogs, they experienced considerable human contact. Dogs used as sheepdogs must undergo substantial training by a shepherd. This relationship makes the dog into a companion to the shepherd, not just a herding tool. More than any other factor, the generations of the shepherd-sheepdog relationship are responsible for the vigilant, obedient, protective, and easy-to-train nature of the Sheltie.

Most of the physical attributes of the Shetland Sheepdog result from generations of selective breeding. During the last century, breeders have also carefully developed the temperament they deemed desirable in sheepdogs and have tried to eliminate unwanted behavioral problems. For instance, having an aggressive sheepdog would be undesirable. This would frighten the sheep just as much as any predator they might encounter. Therefore, a Sheltie breeder would avoid mating any dogs considered aggressive. Thus, breeders have successfully weeded out many inherent canine behaviors that would be undesirable in a herding dog.

In summary, the nature of the Shetland Sheepdog is a blend of three elements. The first includes all instinctive behavior, such as sexual drive, the marking of territories, and the establishment of a ranking order. The second and third elements result from domestication. They include selectively bred traits and people-oriented traits developed from the shepherd-dog relationship.

Behavior Problems

Because of the care and consistency used by Shetland Sheepdog breeders, relatively few behavior problems are encountered in this breed. In recent years, however, as the popularity of the Sheltie increases, we have also seen an increase in poorly bred dogs. These dogs have been mated by unscrupulous breeders who have obtained the cheapest stud dogs, who care little for the advancement of the breed, and who are doing this only to make a profit. Poor breeding practices usually result in dogs that, besides not meeting the physical requirements of the standard, have behavior problems. These problems include shyness, overaggressiveness, or hyperactivity, to name a few.

The major behavior problem associated with the Sheltie is shyness. Although some may not consider shyness in a dog a problem, you must remember that Shelties are herding dogs. Putting a timid dog out in the fields to protect your flock would be ludicrous.

Shyness, however, is not a new problem to the Sheltie breeder. In fact, it dates back to when the dogs were first discovered in the

Dog/Human Age Equivalents

Dog's Age	Human's Age	Dog's Age	Human's Age
2 months	14 months	7 years	49 years
3 months	3 years	8 years	56 years
6 months	5 years	9 years	63 years
8 months	9 years	10 years	65 years
12 months	14 years	11 years	71 years
18 months	20 years	12 years	75 years
2 years	24 years	13 years	80 years
3 years	30 years	14 years	84 years
4 years	36 years	15 years	87 years
5 years	40 years	16 years	89 years
6 years	42 years	17 years	95 years

Shetland Islands. It is believed that in the isolation of the islands, Shelties rarely encountered humans beside their owners. These dogs reacted in one of two ways. They were either cautious and watchful of strangers, or they became timid and moved away. So from early in their history, Sheltie breeders have encountered the unwanted trait of excessive timidity.

As a general practice, quality breeders have avoided breeding shy Shelties, and this problem has always been under control. However, because some breeders are ready to compromise for profit, an increase in shy Shetland Sheepdogs has been seen along with the increase of the breed's popularity.

While detecting some shyness in a Sheltie puppy may be possible, many times the extent of this problem cannot be seen until the dog is older. Therefore, be sure to purchase your dog from a reliable and conscientious breeder. Even if you do this, however, your dog may still develop behavior problems. Sometimes controlling this problem is possible through extensive training and counter-conditioning. If, however, you do find that your Sheltie has any problems, be it shyness, overaggressiveness, or any other abnormal behavior, do not mate your dog. While you may still love your dog, for the sake of the breed do not increase the incidence of these problems.

Your Dog's Signals

All dogs use their voices, body language, and facial expressions to convey their emotions. You must pay special attention to these signals to understand your dog's moods.

Dogs do not make noises without a reason. Each sound reflects a mood. A dog will yelp in fright or pain, whine and whimper in loneliness or when seeking attention, groan in contentment or when ailing, and bark in anger or glee. Often you must look for additional signs to determine the purpose of the sounds.

Body language is also a good indicator of a dog's mood. A joyous dog jumps up and down eagerly and may bark. A dog that crouches and lowers its head to the floor is exhibiting fear of being punished, of an intruder, or of another dog. The best indicator of your dog's emotions, however, is its tail. A happy dog wags its tail briskly. The happier it is, the more briskly its tail wags. A frightened dog puts its tail between its legs. An alert or attentive Sheltie raises its tail slightly, while a contented dog has a lowered tail (but not between its legs).

Finally, watch your Sheltie's ears and muzzle, for they are a primary means of facial expression. A contented Sheltie has a closed mouth and normal-set ears. An alert, aroused, or attentive dog picks up its ears. Often your dog will cock its head inquisitively to one side or the other. Be wary of *any* dog whose ears are back, upper lips are raised, mouth is open, and is growling. Although you will rarely see a Sheltie in this position, remember that these are all warning signals of fear and/or anger, and they may precede an attack.

Sense Organs

Dogs in general rely heavily on the senses of smell, hearing, taste, and touch and less on the sense of sight. Like other features, sense organs in a particular breed have been developed through selective breeding and domestication.

The sense of smell is very important to a Sheltie. This sense enables it to find food, locate a mate, and decipher territories.

The area of the olfactory system concerned with smell is more than 40 times larger in a Sheltie than in humans. In addition, Shelties can remember thousands of odors and can associate them with the appropriate people, animals, and places.

Shelties also possess a highly developed sense of hearing, superior to that of humans. They hear a wider range of sounds, especially high-pitched frequencies, such as those emitted from a Galton whistle (silent dog whistle). Shelties hear sounds from a much greater distance than do humans. Their acute hearing is also important to their usefulness as herding dogs. Many shepherds train their dogs to perform commands at the sound of various whistle codes. They do this because high-pitched whistle sounds can travel farther and even during stormy weather can be heard more clearly by the sheepdog.

Shelties' peripheral vision is much greater than that of humans. However, their eyes do not focus as sharply as do those of humans. As a result, their eyes are much more sensitive to motion. However, they must rely more on smell and sound to interpret what they see.

Because Shelties possess a long, thick, two-layered, weather-resistant coat, their bodies may appear to lack some sensitivity. However, the body parts not covered by this thick coat, such as the muzzle and nose, do seem to have a high degree of feeling.

Like other dogs, Shelties possess other senses that we still do not understand completely. For example, they have an innate sense of direction. We have all heard reports of dogs traveling hundreds of miles to return home.

As Your Puppy Matures

Additional insight into your Sheltie can be gained when you examine the dog's aging process. As your dog goes through the various stages of its life, it will undergo both physical and emotional changes. The first major change will occur when the young puppy is removed from its littermates and placed into what is expected to become its permanent home.

It is important to familiarize your Sheltie with the outside world.

From the time a puppy is born until it is in its seventh week, it leads a quiet and secure life in the presence of its mother, brothers, and sisters. At the point when the puppy is relocated in its new home, it is becoming much more aware of the world around it. A puppy at this age is very curious, mischievous, and also very impressionable. Training serves as a method of satisfying its curiosity and enables the puppy to learn the rules of its new home. Training will also help the puppy differentiate between playtime and serious time.

Around this time in a puppy's life, it is also becoming more aware of its own physical attributes. Even before you bring your puppy home, it will have already begun to have mock fights with its littermates. This serves to build up strength and to improve motor skills.

When you bring your puppy home, you will find that it is both emotionally and physically ready to adapt itself to its new household. Thus, training should begin immediately. If you wait too long, you will allow this impressionable little creature to pick up bad habits, some of which you may never uproot.

By the time your puppy is 12 or 13 weeks old it reaches what I refer to as the questioning stage. The questioning stage for a puppy is similar to that point when a human child asks "Why is the sky blue?" shortly followed by "Why this?" and "Why that?" In your puppy's case, it has become completely aware of itself and its environment. Its favorite pastime will be to share its discoveries with you. It will begin to investigate everything, primarily with its teeth. At this time, it begins to lose its baby teeth and get its permanent ones. Remember that your puppy is still very impressionable, so treat it with care, and continue to reinforce the basic rules of your house.

At seven to ten months old, your puppy will have almost reached its full adult size. This is also when the dog reaches sexual maturity, the equivalent of human adolescence. Its once innocent curiosity will have changed into a bold and assertive interest. This is also a time when, as a teenager might do, your dog begins to test the system. At this point, your Sheltie should be much more comfortable with your lifestyle and will feel it should be included in all your activities. Your Sheltie should know exactly what you expect of it and how it should behave. However, it will naturally try to challenge you to improve its rank. This is, after all, a part of its instinctive canine behavior. When this happens, do not lose your temper. Just teach your Sheltie calmly and firmly that you are the authority. In doing this, you can lead your dog through its final stage of development.

Once your Sheltie reaches maturity, it probably will not undergo any behavioral changes (with the exception of mating urges) until it reaches a ripe old age. Your consistency and evenness of temper in training your dog should now pay off with many years of companionship with a loving, devoted, and trustworthy Shetland Sheepdog.

Changes that occur in the geriatric years depend more on the individual dog and on its medical background. With many old dogs, changes in their daily routines or behavior are often due to a medical problem brought on by old age. As your dog ages, its digestive and immune systems slowly begin to deteriorate. The long-term results can include circulatory, musculoskeletal, and nervous system problems. Thus, your older dog might become lethargic or moody, lose its orientation, or experience hearing loss. It may even forget learned responses.

This may all sound dreadful, but it is simply a part of the aging process. You cannot do much except try to understand.

Outside Encounters

As part of its heritage as a sheepdog, a Sheltie must learn not to fear people. It is normal for a Sheltie to be wary of strangers, but a sheepdog should never display fear. You can help your dog overcome this problem by introducing it to the outside world and the ways of other humans while it is still very young. In addition to removing the feelings of fear, this will also help your dog learn to behave properly when you have visitors.

On occasion, take your dog with you when you shop. Exposure to strange places and people (as long as you accompany it) will help increase the puppy's confidence in itself and in you. Also take the dog on short car trips. Gradually lengthen the trips until the puppy is used to traveling. A familiarity with travel will make future vacations with your dog much more pleasant.

When you travel by car, keep your dog in a small cage to prevent it from getting in your way and to protect it from injury from sudden stops. You should never leave your dog in the car in hot weather. Even with the windows open, heat builds up very rapidly and can result in heatstroke and death.

In order to truly familiarize your puppy with the ways of the world, walk it (on a leash) in areas where you are likely to encounter other humans and other dogs as well. Allow your puppy to have contact with other humans, as long as that person does not mind. As the teacher, you must show no hesitation toward an approaching stranger. Sometimes your dog can sense this hesitation and will interpret it as a reason to shy away.

When any two dogs encounter each other, they will inevitably try to establish a ranking order. In most cases, this is determined through a mock fight (usually looking like playful wrestling) whereby one dog ends up lying on its back in a subordinate position. However, if neither dog is willing to back down, a real fight might ensue, so be prepared for this possibility. If either dog displays a threatening posture or growls in anger, remove your dog immediately.

If you should encounter another dog, restrain your puppy until the strange dog approaches it. If the two dogs wag their tails and then sniff each other's nose and tail, you can assume that they like each other. Encourage your Sheltie to play with the other dog. Playing will make your Sheltie feel more comfortable in strange surroundings.

BASIC AND ADVANCED TRAINING

Like almost all of the herding dogs, Shetland Sheepdogs are relatively easy to train. This is because the hundreds of years of shepherd-dog relationships have imprinted the Sheltie with an innate willingness to learn. For this reason, you can begin to train a Sheltie at a much earlier age than many other breeds. In addition, if you conduct your training program properly, you will be able to keep your Sheltie puppy's attention for a longer period of time, thus leading to quicker learning.

Bear in mind that this chapter does not describe all the skills a Sheltie can learn. In fact, I believe that if you have the time, patience, and energy, you can teach your Sheltie an endless number of skills. You must, however, be able to communicate your ideas to your eager student.

Why Dogs Learn

Dogs are pack animals. Because they hunt and live as a group, dogs must learn to coexist in order to survive. This coexistence depends on ranking order. Each dog has a place in the ranking order, usually based on strength and experience. In the pack, all dogs submit to a dog of higher authority. Similarly, a domesticated dog submits only to a higher ranking authority.

The Shelties' herding instinct makes them easily trainable dogs.

Through training, a puppy learns that you are the authority and that the other members of your family rank higher than it does. In addition to establishing ranking order, training teaches your puppy the rules of your house. Teaching a puppy actions and behaviors that are not instinctive takes patience, understanding, and love. You must be consistent and authoritative yet must never lose your temper. Try to understand that human ways are unfamiliar to your Sheltie puppy but that it is eager to learn. Your puppy depends on you to find the proper way to teach it. Once you find the right method, your puppy will respond eagerly and joyfully.

Basic Training Rules

The ten rules listed here will help to set up a good training program for your Sheltie puppy. Each time you begin a training session, make sure you adhere to these rules. This will assure that you give your puppy the best chance to learn its lessons as thoroughly and rapidly as possible.

1. Begin working with your puppy the day you bring it home. Hold two or three sessions a day, and hold them for as long as the puppy shows interest. In 10 or 15 minutes, you can provide sufficient teaching without boring the dog. Your puppy may need two weeks or longer to begin understanding some of your commands, so do not neglect your training.

2. Be consistent. All of the members of your household must decide what is permitted behavior and what is not. For instance, one person should not be teaching the dog to beg for food while the others are teaching the dog not to hang around the dinner table. Once your dog has learned a lesson, never allow it to do the contrary without a reprimand.

3. Be authoritative. Your dog will understand tones better than words. You must deliver all visual and verbal commands clearly and unmistakably. Reprimands must be sharp and firm, while praise must be calm and friendly. While the dog must learn that you are in charge, never demonstrate your authority by using physical force. In addition to being totally unnecessary, forcing your dog to perform or hitting it will teach your dog only to dislike its training sessions.

4. Hold each training session in an atmosphere conducive to learning. Be sure there are as few distractions as possible, and never attempt to teach your puppy anything when you are in a bad mood. Your negative attitude will only confuse the puppy and make learning harder.

5. Do not attempt to teach your puppy more than one new lesson in a single session, and never move to a new concept until the dog has mastered the previous one. Puppies, like people, learn at their own pace and should never be rushed. Once a lesson has been mastered, it can be included as a warm-up exercise in your dog's training regimen.

6. Praise your dog generously for its successes. Verbal praise, petting, or scratching behind the ears will make your Sheltie an eager student. Although trainers often reward their pupils with food, this practice is not necessary. Enthusiastic praise should be enough incentive for your puppy to perform correctly.

7. Punish disobedience immediately. Since a puppy has a very short memory, you must never put off a reprimand. If, for example, your puppy chews a slipper, do not punish it unless you catch it in the act; otherwise it will not understand why you are displeased. An adult dog that knows better, however, can be disciplined for the same offense after showing it the slipper.

8. Limit punishments to verbal reprimands. In extreme cases, you can confine your dog to its cage after giving it a verbal reprimand.

9. Even when your dog is older, keep your training sessions short. End them early if the dog begins to lose interest.

10. Never hold a training session when your dog is tired. A tired or exhausted dog will not be attentive. Make it a practice to hold your training sessions before you feed your Sheltie, as it will be less likely to be sleepy or sluggish.

Puppy Training

As previously mentioned, training begins the day you bring your puppy home. The longer you wait, the more difficult it will be for your puppy to learn. First teach your Sheltie its name. If you always address your puppy by name, you will be amazed at how fast it will learn this lesson. Make sure your Sheltie does not hear nicknames. This will confuse it, and it will not respond when called.

Another important lesson is the meaning of "No." Your puppy will probably have to begin learning this lesson its first day at home. As your puppy first explores your home, it will probably do something wrong. When it does, tell it *"No"* in a sharp, firm tone that shows you are serious. If your puppy refuses to listen, pick it up and place it into its cage. *Never* hit your puppy, either with your hand or with a rolled newspaper, for this will make your puppy hand-shy. Using a cage will simplify training. In addition, as you will see later, it will also speed the process of housebreaking.

Being Alone

A puppy must learn early that it will be left alone on occasion. You must teach it to behave properly while you are away, for a poorly trained puppy can cause great damage.

To accustom your puppy to being alone, leave it in a familiar room. Then go into another room where the puppy can neither see nor hear you. Stay there for a short while and then return. If your puppy has done anything wrong, reprimand it. Gradually increase the time you leave the dog in the room alone.

If you must leave before you can trust your puppy alone, lock it in its cage with food, water, and toys until you return. If you do not have a cage, lock it in a familiar room. Remove all tempting objects, including shoes, papers, and clothing. Make sure you leave the puppy its bed and an ample supply of food, water, and toys.

Do not leave a very young puppy alone in your yard, where too many uncontrollable factors exist. Children may tease the puppy, and other animals may be able to bother or hurt it.

No Begging Allowed

To some people, seeing a dog beg looks like a cute and innocent act. Unfortunately, begging is a bad habit for a puppy to develop, and it should never be condoned. Begging may start very innocently. You will be sitting down at the table, about to begin eating a thick steak, when you notice something out of the corner of your eye. It is your faithful puppy, waiting patiently nearby, staring at you with pleading eyes. Now is when most people make their big mistake. They will call the dog over and reward it with a table scrap. You would be amazed at how such a simple act could turn into a nasty habit. While having your Sheltie as a constant table companion may not bother you, it may bother others who are guests in your house.

If your Sheltie attempts to beg for scraps, you must scold it with a sharp *"No!"* and point away from the table and toward the puppy's cage or sleeping box. Within a few weeks, your puppy will learn to avoid the table during mealtimes.

Walking on a Leash

You should start to teach your puppy how to walk on a leash from the first day you bring it home. Before you even bring the puppy into your home, you will be taking it for a walk around your yard to let it relieve itself. Place a collar on the puppy, making sure it is neither too tight nor too loose. Attach a leash, and take your puppy for its first walk. Hold the leash on your left side, and use gentle persuasion to keep your puppy close to your leg. Do not allow the puppy to get under your feet, and do not let it run ahead of you. Remain patient. A Sheltie puppy's legs are very short, and the dog is not capable of tremendous speed. If your puppy falls behind, do not attempt to drag it forward. Use friendly words, patience, and a little bit of gentle force to keep your puppy in its proper walking position.

Unnecessary Barking

Barking is one of the most common problems of canine behavior. It is, of course, a natural response for almost all dogs. Even though barking may have numerous causes, including behavioral problems, this section deals with some corrective approaches you can take to help break bad learned behaviors.

Barking is often the sign of alarm. Because of this, you may not want to curb any of your Sheltie's watchdog tendencies. Therefore, discovering whether any of your dog's bad barking habits are an inherited problem or a learned behavior is important. (Inherited problems are discussed in the Understanding Shelties chapter, page 70.)

A learned behavior, for example, is one where the dog barks upon hearing the command *"Speak."* If a dog has been trained by getting food after it speaks, then a dog may speak on its own in order to get a reward. This habit can be broken by *never* giving a dog a reward after it is told to speak. This method is called extinction and relies on the trainer repeating the command over and over but never, ever giving the dog a reward (outside of verbal praise and petting).

This type of training is normally very effective in stopping any bad learned behaviors (such as barking to get into or out of the house, barking to receive food or attention, and so forth). However, be warned. Breaking such bad habits may take a lot of time and patience.

Simple Commands

The first commands to teach your dog are *sit, stay, come,* and *heel.* Teach these commands using these words, and not phrases like *"Come over here, Sparky."* Your dog does not understand complete sentences but rather relies on the command word, your tone, and your gesture. Do not try to teach your Sheltie these commands for long periods of time. Training for short periods two or three times a day is better. Train before you feed the dog, because afterward it may be sluggish. Also, make sure to walk the dog before training. To avoid distractions, train your puppy in a confined area without an audience.

Sit: Take your puppy into an isolated room and fit it with a collar and leash. Hold the leash with your right hand, and place your left hand

Consistency is crucial when training your puppy.

If you must leave your puppy alone, lock it in its cage.

onto the puppy's hindquarters. Then give the command *"Sit!"* or *"Sit, Sparky!"* in a firm voice, at the same time pressing gently and steadily on its hindquarters. Gently pull the leash upward to keep your puppy from lying down on the floor. Hold the dog in this position for a while. Do not allow it to jump back up.

Do not expect your Sheltie to master this command after the first training session. Repeat the procedure for the entire session or until the puppy begins to lose interest. Remember to praise its efforts each time it sits properly. If you repeat the procedure every day, your Sheltie will soon learn this command.

Once your puppy has performed the sit at least a couple of times in succession, remove the leash and give the command. If your dog has been properly trained, it will perform correctly. If not, remain patient and try again with the leash on.

If you want to use your Sheltie for herding, teach it to respond to a hand signal and to whistles as well. In the field, your dog may be at a distance where it can see you but not hear you. This way your dog can understand your command even if noise prevents it from hearing you. In addition, the sharp sounds of whistles are easier than verbal commands for your dog to hear and interpret from a distance. Once your puppy has mastered the command, hold up either your hand or a single finger in a distinct gesture, and say *"Sit,"* making sure the dog can see the signal. Always use the word (or sound) and the gesture together so your dog connects the two.

Stay: This is a more difficult command to teach your puppy, for it will always want to be at your side. The *stay* command orders your dog to remain still wherever it is. This command may someday save your dog's life.

In teaching your dog to stay, first fit it with a leash and collar. Then run through the *sit* procedure and follow it with the command *"Stay."* As you say this new command, raise your hand, palm toward the dog, like a police officer stopping traffic. Each time your dog attempts to stand up, reproach it with a sharp *"No!"*

Take up all the slack in the leash to hold your dog in place. Repeat the procedure until the dog appears to understand. Then remove the leash and repeat the command several times. Praise the dog each time it obeys. If it disobeys, reprimand it.

Continue this command until your Sheltie has repeated the act with regular success. Then, slowly back away from the dog, making sure to maintain eye contact. While you are moving backward, keep repeating the word *"Stay."* The verbal command should be accompanied by the proper hand gesture. If your Sheltie attempts to follow, give it a loud, sharp *"Stay!"* If the dog continues to follow you, reprimand it. Of course, a dog that stays when told deserves great praise. The *stay* command is sometimes difficult for a devoted puppy to obey because it will always have the urge to be by your side.

Come: If you call out your puppy's name, it will probably race across the room to greet you. The trick to the *come* command, however, is to have your Sheltie obediently come to you when something of greater interest is attracting its attention. *Come* is another command that can protect your dog from dangerous situations.

You should teach the command *come* to your puppy right after *sit* and *stay*. Start by running through the *sit* and *stay* procedures. Once it has stayed at a good distance, call the dog by name and follow with the command, *"Sparky, come!"* Accompany your words with a lively sound or gesture like clapping your hands or slapping your thighs. This will help to excite your dog into motion.

Your Sheltie will quickly associate the word *come* with your movements. Praise it for responding correctly. If it does not respond to the command, put it on a long rope, and let it wander off. Then slowly reel in the rope while repeating the word *"Come!"* Shower your dog with praise when it reaches you. Repeat this exercise several times; then try it without the rope again. Luckily, most Shelties never require this rope exercise.

Obedience Training

The obedience exercises are important for several reasons. Each of the exercises is a requirement for your dog to perform should you enter it into an Obedience competition. However, some of the lessons, such as heeling or relinquishing an object, are important for all dogs to learn. They will allow you to handle your dog properly in awkward situations and will help to reinforce your dog's understanding of the master/subordinate relationship.

Obedience Schools

Contrary to popular belief, obedience schools are not schools for wayward dogs. Instead, they are where, in the proper atmosphere, your dog can learn all it must know to compete in shows. Even if you do not plan to enter your Sheltie into an Obedience trial, these schools offer an enjoyable, interesting, and easy alternative to training your dog alone. These schools are run by experienced dog handlers who can supply you with expert advice and invaluable training tips.

An older child in the family should be the one to take your Sheltie to obedience classes. This allows the child and dog to spend more time together. It also teaches your child how to care for a dog responsibly. Working with a dog at obedience school will teach your child both greater self-respect and respect for the dog.

Check with your Shetland Sheepdog Club and the AKC for a reputable obedience school in your area. Before enrolling your dog, make sure the class suits your purpose. Most schools offer special classes for owners interested in showing their dogs, and others for amateurs. Remember that obedience schools can be costly, depending on the problems your dog presents.

Heeling

When your Sheltie heels properly, it will walk on your left with its head about the same distance forward as your knees. When you begin teaching your dog this lesson, you will require the leash. Eventually, your Sheltie must learn to heel without the restraint of the leash.

To start, run through all the other commands your dog has mastered. This will give your dog extra confidence before you start this difficult lesson. Hold the end of the leash in your right hand, and grab about halfway toward the collar with your left hand. Begin a brisk walk (by your dog's standard) giving the sharp command *"Heel"* or *"Heel, Sparky!"* Use your left hand to control and guide. With this new command, your dog may act rather unpredictably at first, but be patient.

If your dog lags behind, pull steadily on the leash to bring it even with your leg. Do not drag the dog forward or force it to obey your commands, for this will destroy the well-established learning atmosphere. If your dog runs forward, pull it back to your side and give the *heel* command again. If you have difficulty getting your dog to perform correctly, run through the old *sit* and *stay* exercises. Whenever your dog responds correctly, praise it. When it reacts improperly, reprimand it immediately. When it has performed the *sit* and *stay* correctly, begin the *heel* exercises again.

The *heel* lesson is very difficult for a dog to learn. Take your time, be patient, and do not try to teach your dog too quickly. Once your Sheltie has mastered the *heel* on a leash, take it through a turning exercise. If it has trouble heeling while you turn, then take a shorter grip on the leash, and bring the dog closer to your side. Then repeat the command *heel* in a sharp tone, and gently persuade it to follow you by lightly pulling on the leash. As your Sheltie improves in this lesson, take it through a series of straight line, right turn, and left turn exercises. Once it has mastered turning, you can begin training with a slack leash.

Go through the heeling exercises with the leash exerting no pressure on your dog's collar. At the dog's first mistake, grasp the leash firmly and lead the dog steadily in the proper direction. When your dog performs correctly, remember to praise it.

When your dog has learned to walk correctly with a slack leash, remove the leash completely. If it has performed properly with a loose leash, you should be able to achieve the same results without the leash. Do not allow your Sheltie to regress into any bad habits. If the dog does not perform properly, then verbally reprimand it. If you continue to have trouble, you will have to put the leash back on. Repeat the *heel* lesson, then try again without the leash. If you repeat the lessons carefully, and have the exact same routine with and without the leash, your dog should eventually learn to heel properly. Always remember to praise a job well done. This will help to reinforce your Sheltie's good behavior.

Relinquishing an Object

Every good dog must learn to give up any object obediently, if its master so desires. Shelties are no exception. This lesson is important in teaching your dog its subordinate role.

Begin by giving your Sheltie a suitably sized piece of nonsplintering wood to hold in its teeth. Then command your dog to sit, praising it when it obeys. While using both hands, slowly pull the dog's jaws apart while saying *"Let go"* in a strict and firm tone. If your dog begins to growl, give it a sharp *"No!"* Do not be afraid if your Sheltie growls. This is a dog's way of trying to establish its dominance and a natural reaction to anyone who attempts to take away its prey. You must, however, make your Sheltie clearly understand that you are the boss, and take the object away. Once your dog accepts you as a dominant force, it will give up the stick without any objection.

Lying Down

Have your dog assume a sitting position (which should be easy by now). Then slowly pull its front legs forward while saying *"Down!"* If your dog attempts to stand up, give it a sharp *"No!"* If pulling on its front legs does not work, then slowly pull them forward and push

down on the dog's shoulders at the same time. While you do this give the command *"Down!"* Because you will have both hands occupied, you can carefully step on the leash to prevent the dog from returning to its feet. Keep the dog in the lying position for about one minute. Gradually increase this time period as your dog progresses. When your dog has mastered this lesson, begin to move away. As you do this, you must maintain constant eye contact with your pupil. Whenever the dog attempts to stand up, repeat the command *"Down!"* in a firm, sharp tone. Repeat the lesson until you are satisfied with your Sheltie's performance.

Retrieving

Retrieving is an unusual act for any Shetland Sheepdog to perform. However, you may be surprised at the number of Shelties who perform this feat as if it were instinctive. On the other hand, I have met several other Shelties that would attempt to herd a ball back to its owner by encircling it and barking rather than picking it up in its mouth and returning it obediently.

With proper training, any young Sheltie can learn the art of retrieving. Throw a suitably sized nonedible ball or stick, with your dog standing next to you, and call out *"Fetch."* Provided that you did not throw the object clear out of the dog's sight, it will most likely run after the object.

If the dog picks up the object in its mouth and returns to you, command the dog to sit,

Sit and stay are two of the most important commands you can teach your Sheltie. If a dog learns no other commands but these, you can still keep it out of numerous harmful situations.

Although this Sheltie looks like it's taking a break, it is in fact being trained to sit in place at an elevated height. This allows sheepdogs to spot danger at a greater distance and to guard their flock better.

put out your hand, palm up, under its lower jaw, and say, *"Let go!"* You should be able to remove the object from the dog's mouth without any resistance. If your dog drops the object, place it back into its mouth, and then remove it, saying *"Let go!"*

If your Sheltie shows no desire to return with the object, repeat the exercise using a 30-foot (9 m) rope. Tie the dog to the cord, throw the object, and call out *"Fetch!"* again. Once it has picked up the object, draw the dog toward you. Then take the object from the dog.

If your dog hesitates in picking up the object, place the object into its mouth and follow the commands for relinquishing an object. Keep repeating this lesson until the dog understands that it must take this object into its mouth. Then throw the object only a short distance to see if the dog will pick it up. With patience and persistence, you can teach your Sheltie to perform this command as well as if it were a Retriever bringing a hunter its prey.

Jumping Over Hurdles

This may not be as difficult a lesson as you may think (provided the hurdles are Sheltie sized). Herding dogs must know how to jump over obstacles, if need be, to prevent a flock from scattering. You may find that your dog will learn this lesson with relative ease. First, command your dog to sit on one side of a small pile of boards while you stand on the opposite side. Command the dog by saying, *"Jump!"* If it walks around the obstacle, say *"No!"* then bring it back and start over. Praise your dog for a successful performance.

As your dog learns to jump over the hurdle on command, gradually increase the obstacle's height. Be careful not to make the jump too high, for this can hurt young dogs and discourage further jumping.

Once your dog has learned to jump on command, begin a jump and retrieve exercise. Place the object to be retrieved on the other side of the hurdle. Command your dog to sit next to you. Then command it to retrieve the object by saying, *"Jump! Fetch!"* in a clear, firm voice. The dog should leap over the obstacle, pick up the object, and jump back with it. Tell the dog to sit again. Then take the object out of its mouth by saying," *Let go!"* Praise your dog warmly for its accomplishments.

Problems in Training

No two Shetland Sheepdogs are precisely alike. Each has its own idiosyncrasies. Individual learning abilities can vary greatly. The key in training is to establish the proper rapport with your dog. As I have stated earlier, the training exercises described in this book are merely outlines for teaching commands. You have the responsibility, as your dog's trainer, to establish an effective system of communication. This will make it easier for your Sheltie to understand your commands and perform them well.

If you reach a point when your Sheltie has trouble learning a lesson, remain patient and understanding. Never try to force your Sheltie to learn. Anger and beating have never helped a dog learn anything! They only serve to create an atmosphere not conducive to learning. Eventually, this will cause your Sheltie to lose trust in you.

When you and your pupil hit a roadblock, start by examining your teaching methods. Review the ten basic rules of training (page 77), and correct any mistakes that you may have been making. In most cases, you will find that your teaching method was causing the problem.

If, after thoroughly reviewing your methods, you feel that this is not the problem, carefully examine your dog and its environment. Your Sheltie could possibly be distracted by an outside factor. If so, then you must remove the distraction. Could your dog be ill? If illness is suspected, make an appointment to see your veterinarian.

Should you continue to run into training difficulties, I strongly recommend that you contact a reputable obedience school. In many instances, the human ego will not allow us to believe that we could be doing anything wrong. Professional dog handlers who run these training facilities can usually spot problems rather easily.

By starting early and working hard, you will most assuredly be able to train your Sheltie to whatever stage you desire. Only as you grow older with your Sheltie will you begin to understand the importance of proper training and begin to reap its rewards. Through diligence and the establishment of a harmonious training atmosphere, you and your faithful four-legged companion will enjoy many wonderful years of camaraderie.

Dog Shows and Exhibitions

A purebred such as the Shetland Sheepdog may be entered into any *dog show* or Obedience competition. These licensed shows are conducted under rules established by the AKC. The term *dog show* usually refers to a bench competition in which a Shetland Sheepdog is judged on appearance, physique, bearing, and temperament. In these events, a dog is judged strictly on how it conforms to the standard for that particular breed as compared with all the other dogs entered in the competition.

At Obedience trials a Sheltie is judged entirely on performance in a series of exercises. These exercises, chosen beforehand by the AKC, are based upon any work the dog may be required to do. The exercises to be performed are based on the dog's experience in the Obedience ring and may include heel on leash, heel free, recall, long sit, retrieve on flat or over high jump, broad jump, scent discrimination, or a signal exercise.

Another type of exhibition sponsored by the AKC is the field trial. However, these competitions are designed for hunting dogs, such as Spaniels or Retrievers. Most of the events in a field trial are designed to simulate actual hunting conditions and, as such, make it impossible for a herding dog such as the Sheltie to compete fairly.

The good news for Shetland Sheepdog owners is that the AKC does sponsor Herding trials. Competing in these trials will allow you and your Sheltie to compete for six different Herding titles, which, when earned, will be shown on your dog's pedigree papers. The titles are classified as HT for Herding Tested, PT for Pre-trial, HS for Herding Started, HI for Herding Intermediate, HX for Herding Advanced, and H.Ch for Herding Champion.

Herding Tested and Pre-trial competitions are called test titles, and are performed on a pass/fail basis. To qualify for these titles, your Sheltie must have two qualifying runs under two separate judges. An HT trial is held in an area with a minimum size of 100 by 100 feet (30 by 30 m) for sheep herding (a smaller area is used for herding ducks), and the handler will enter with the dog on a lead. The handler must place the dog into a *stay* position (the *sit, stand,* or *down* positions are all acceptable), and the lead is to be removed. The dog must then maneuver sheep from the starting point to a marker then back to the starting point. This is repeated three times. The dog must demonstrate controlled movement during the entire exercise. At the end the handler must stop the dog and recall it to the starting point. During the trial, which has a 10-minute time limit, the handler is to command the dog using verbal commands or whistles. The dog (and handler) are to be judged on five elements: the controlled pause at the start, the controlled movement during the first set of directional changes, the controlled movement during the second set, the stop, and the recall.

Pre-trial competitions are held on a larger field. The dog is commanded to move the stock through a series of four gates and into a pen. For these trials, the dog is judged on a controlled stay at the start, the controlled passage through the four gates, one stop on the course, one stop near the pen while the handler opens the gate, and penning the stock.

Herding Started, Intermediate, and Advanced competitions are called trial titles. They differ from the test title competitions in that several different type of courses can be set up, all of which have obstacles. The location of the

As soon as the simple commands are mastered, you can teach your Sheltie many other skills such as negotiating obstacles. This training is extremely important if you plan to compete in formal Herding or Obedience trials.

The intelligence of this breed and its hereditary herding instincts make it possible to teach a Sheltie practically any skill. This clever Sheltie is mastering the traversing of a seesaw.

obstacles depends on the type of course and the skill level at which the dogs are competing. The trial title courses are much larger than those used for test titles, and the time limits are greater as well. In these trials, the herding dog earns points in several different judging categories instead of earning a pass/fail score. To be successful, the Sheltie must perform all of the skills required and earn at least half of the points available for each category. The dog must also earn an overall score of 60 points or better out of a possible 100 points to advance to the next level. The description of the different courses, the judging categories, and the point system is too lengthy for this book, However, if you are interested in getting more information and a set of rules for Herding competition, you can obtain them from the AKC.

The trainer follows through for the descent of the ramp.

Because bench competitions, Obedience competitions, and Herding trials each have a different format, you should attend them to learn more about judging. Also, these competitions offer dog owners a wide variety of helpful information. Manufacturers of dog food and other pet products often attend and sometimes display their merchandise. You will also be able to exchange tips with other dog owners and breeders. Often the judges advise owners about the care and grooming of their dogs.

If you wish to enter your dog into a show, check with your local Shetland Sheepdog Club.

They can advise you about the event, help you obtain and complete the application form, and inform you of the entry fee. Prior to the show, you must supply the judges with your dog's pedigree, certificate of health, and an International Certificate of Immunization.

Whether you enter your Sheltie or not, attending a dog show is a rewarding and educational experience. If you do decide to enter your dog, do not count on its winning or achieving a good score. Remember that dog show judges are very strict. Your Sheltie may not meet their interpretation of the standard. If this is the case, just enjoy the show and the experience of owning a purebred dog.

HOW–TO: HOUSEBREAKING

Housebreaking a puppy has never been considered a lot of fun for the dog owner. Certain methods, however, can speed up the process.

Paper Training

The objective of paper training is to get your puppy to urinate and defecate on newspapers spread out in an area of your choosing. Naturally, you should choose an area that is easy to clean such as a kitchen or bathroom. Make sure that the area you choose is not too close to your puppy's eating or sleeping areas. Your Sheltie will instinctively try to keep those areas clean and will not excrete near them.

Start by confining your puppy to the area you have chosen until it voids. If it used the paper, remove the top soiled sheet, and place fresh, clean papers under what were formerly the bottom sheets. By doing this, you will be leaving the scent from the bottom papers exposed so that the puppy can relocate the area to repeat the act.

If the puppy misses the paper on its first attempt, get the scent of the dog's urine onto a sheet of newspaper and place it on top of the other sheets. Then thoroughly clean the area where the accident occurred. Removing all scent from the inappropriate area is important so the Sheltie will not become confused by finding its scent in two different locations the next time it has to relieve itself.

Try to remember that after eating, drinking, playing, or waking up, your puppy will probably need to empty its bladder and bowels. Young puppies need to relieve themselves every few hours. Oftentimes the only sign your puppy will give you is that it will begin sniffing the ground, searching for the right place to do its duty. Pick up the puppy, and place it onto the newspaper in the designated area of your home. You can then gently restrain the puppy's movements until it has relieved itself on the paper. Be sure to praise your puppy after it has used the paper.

Cage Training

Cage or crate training offers a faster and easier alternative to paper training. It takes advantage of your puppy's instincts to keep its sleeping area clean. If your puppy is wary on its first encounter with the cage, make the cage more appealing by placing some toys inside. After you confine the puppy to its cage a few times with its excreta, it will quickly learn to restrain itself until you let it out of its cage. Naturally, you must take the puppy outdoors to relieve itself as soon as you let it out of the cage. Establish a time schedule for letting the Sheltie

Housebreaking can be made easier if you put some of your puppy's scent on the paper being used. A puppy will rely more on smell than sight to locate the area where it should relieve itself.

out to relieve itself. As your puppy becomes more used to the schedule, you can let it out of its cage for longer periods of time. Eventually, you will be able to leave the cage door open at all times without fear of accidents.

Using a cage has additional benefits. Before domestication, dogs were cave-dwelling animals. Instinctively, the modern dog finds security in any cavelike structure once it becomes familiar with it. If you use a cage, your dog will prefer to sleep there and will return on its own. The cage can therefore be used as a housebreaking aid, sleeping area, and traveling crate.

The cage can also serve as an invaluable training tool. If your puppy refuses to listen to your commands, you can pick it up and put it into its cage. When your Sheltie becomes involuntarily separated from its family, it will quickly learn that you are not happy with its performance.

Outdoor Training

Outdoor training begins when you first bring your puppy home. Before taking it indoors, take it for a walk in the area where you want it to eliminate. Give your puppy plenty of time to do its duty, and be sure to praise it for a job well done. Verbal praise and petting will help build your puppy's confidence and will increase your chances of future successful performances.

Most puppies need to relieve themselves as many as six times a day, so you will need to take your puppy outdoors about once every three to four hours. Walking the puppy after each of its meals is also advisable. A puppy's stomach will exert additional pressure on the bladder, so do not wait too long. You should take your puppy for its last walk as late in the evening as possible so that your Sheltie puppy is less likely to have accidents during the night. If you continue to bring your puppy to the same area each time, it will eventually seek out this area on its own.

The cage or crate is very useful as a housebreaking aid.

Cleaning Up

While canine droppings are aesthetically unpleasant, it is your responsibility to clean up the mess. Many towns and cities have made it illegal *not* to clean up after your pet.

Wherever you walk your Sheltie, carry a plastic bag or pooper scooper with you. Dispose of the mess in its proper place. When cleaning your garden or yard, pick up and dispose of the droppings in well-sealed plastic bags in a sealed garbage can. For accidents that happen in the home, clean with an odor-eliminating disinfectant. Do not use ammonia because the smell may remind your puppy of its urine.

Accidents Will Happen

If you discover that while you slept, your Sheltie puppy could no longer control itself, remember that this *was an accident.* Getting angry or administering punishment will not do you or your puppy any good. Puppies have very short memories. If you do not catch your puppy in the act or make the discovery shortly afterward, a scolding will only confuse your pet.

International Kennel Clubs

American Shetland Sheepdog Association*
Carol Williamson, Membership Chairperson
9714 Cedarvale
Houston, TX 77055
Lynn Krivenek, Corresponding Secretary
3010 Sentinal Heights Road
La Fayette, NY 13084-9628
Web site: www.assa.ord
e-mail: dundee3@aol.com

American Kennel Club
260 Madison Avenue
New York, NY 10016
Web site: www.akc.org/library.htm
e-mail: info@akc.org

Australian National Kennel Club
Royal Show Grounds
Ascot Vale
Victoria
Australia
Web site: www.ankc.aust.com
e-mail: office@vca.org.au

Canadian Kennel Club
89 Skyway Avenue, Suite 100
Etobicoke, Ontario M9W 6R4
Canada
Web site: www.ckc.ca
e-mail: information@ckc.ca

The Kennel Club
1-5 Clargis Street
Picadilly
London, W1Y 8AB
England
Web site: www.the-kennel-club.org.uk
e-mail: info@the-kennel-club.org.uk

Magazines

Dog Fancy
P.O. Box 6050
Mission Viejo, CA 92690
Web site: www.catfancy.com/dogs/default.asp
e-mail: dogfancy@fancypubs.com

Dogs Monthly
Ascot House 1
High Street
Ascot Berkshire SL5 7JG
England
Web site: www.corsini.co.uk/dogsmonthly

*This address may change as a new officer is elected. The latest listing can always be obtained from the American Kennel Club.

Books

Alderton, David. *The Dog Care Manual.* Barron's Educational Series, Hauppauge, New York, 1986.

Baer, Ted. *Communicating with Your Dog.* Barron's Educational Series, Hauppauge, New York, 1999.

Klever, Ulrich. *The Complete Book of Dog Care.* Barron's Educational Series, Hauppauge, New York, 1989.

Lorenz, Konrad Z. *Man Meets Dog.* Penguin Books, London and New York, 1967.

Rice, Dan. *The Dog Handbook.* Barron's Educational Series, Hauppauge, New York, 1999.

Touring with Towser: a directory of hotels and motels that accommodate guests with dogs. Gaines TWT, P.O. Box 8172, Kankakee, Illinois 60901.

About the Author

Jaime J. Sucher is Director of Research and Development for a manufacturer of pet products. He is the author of *Golden Retrievers* and *Shih Tzu* and has written numerous articles on pet nutrition.

Photo Credits

Norvia Behling: pages 2–3, 8, 9, 17 (bottom right), 24, 36 (top), 40, 44, 52, 64, 80, 81, 92; Tara Darling: pages 12, 32, 36 (bottom), 37, 56, 69, 76, 93; Susan Green: pages 4, 16, 17 (top, bottom left), 20, 25, 29, 48, 49, 60, 61, 68, 73, 84, 85, 88, 89

Cover Photos

Front cover: Susan Green; inside front cover, back cover, inside back cover: Norvia Behling

© Copyright 2000, 1990 by Barron's Educational Series, Inc.

All inquiries should be addressed to:
Barron's Educational Series, Inc.
250 Wireless Boulevard
Hauppauge, NY 11788
http://www.barronseduc.com

Library of Congress Catalog Card No. 99-43591

International Standard Book No. 0-7641-1044-6

Important Note

This book is concerned with selecting, keeping, and raising Shetland Sheepdogs. The publisher and the author think it is important to point out that the advice and information for Shetland Sheepdog maintenance applies to healthy, normally developed animals. Anyone who acquires an adult dog or one from an animal shelter must consider that the animal may have behavioral problems and may, for example, bite without any visible provocation. Such anxiety biters are dangerous for the owner as well as the general public.

Caution is further advised in the association of children with dogs, in meetings with other dogs, and in exercising the dog without a leash.

Library of Congress Cataloging-in-Publication Data
Sucher, Jaime J.
    Shetland sheepdogs : everything about purchase, care, nutrition, breeding, and health care / Jaime J. Sucher.
        p. cm. — (A Complete pet owner's manual)
    Includes bibliographical references (p.) and index.
    ISBN 0-7641-1044-6 (pbk.)
    1. Shetland sheepdog. I. Title. II. Series.
SF429.S62S83   2000
636.737—dc21   99-43591
                                                CIP

Printed in Hong Kong

9 8 7 6 5 4 3